LEADER'S GUIDE

Dr. Justo González, writer of this study resource, was born in Havana, Cuba, the son of two Methodist ministers. He completed his S.T.B. at Union Theological Seminary in Matanzas, Cuba, and then came to the United States to pursue graduate studies in theology. He obtained his Ph.D. in historical theology from Yale University. Since that time, he has held teaching positions at the Evangelical Seminary of Puerto Rico and Candler School of Theology. Although he now teaches on an occasional basis, he is a full-time writer and lecturer.

His books, originally written in either Spanish or English, have been translated into several other languages. He has also written numerous United Methodist curriculum materials as well as materials for other denominations.

LUKE
Copyright © 1994 by Cokesbury
All rights reserved.

JOURNEY THROUGH THE BIBLE: LUKE. LEADER'S GUIDE. An official resource for The United Methodist Church prepared by the General Board of Discipleship through the Division of Church School Publications and published by Cokesbury, a division of The United Methodist Publishing House, 201 Eighth Avenue, South, P. O. Box 801, Nashville, Tennessee 37202. Printed in the United States of America.

Scripture quotations in this publication, unless otherwise indicated, are from the New Revised Standard Version of the Bible, copyrighted © 1989 by the Division of Christian Education of the National Council of the Churches of Christ in the United States of America, and are used by permission. All rights reserved.

For permission to reproduce any material in this publication, call 1-615-749-6421, or write to Cokesbury, Syndication—Permissions Office, 201 Eighth Avenue, South, P. O. Box 801, Nashville, Tennessee 37202.

To orders copies of this publication, call toll free: 1-800-672-1789. Call Monday–Friday, 7:30–5:00 Central Time or 8:30–4:30 Pacific Time. Use your Cokesbury account, American Express, Visa, Discover, or MasterCard.

EDITORIAL TEAM

Debra G. Ball-Kilbourne,
Editor

Linda H. Leach,
Assistant Editor

Linda O. Spicer,
Adult Section Assistant

DESIGN TEAM

Susan J. Scruggs,
Design Supervisor,
Cover Design

Ed Wynne,
Layout Designer

ADMINISTRATIVE STAFF

Neil M. Alexander,
Vice-President, Publishing

Duane A. Ewers,
Editor of Church School Publications

Gary L. Ball-Kilbourne,
Executive Editor of Adult Publications

 Cokesbury

D1709340

07 08 09 10 – 10 9 8 7 6 5

#

| Volume 11: Luke | by Justo L. González |

$\mathcal{I}$NTRODUCTION TO THE SERIES

The leader's guides provided for use with JOURNEY THROUGH THE BIBLE make the following assumptions:

- adults learn in different ways:
  - —by reading
  - —by listening to speakers
  - —by working on projects
  - —by drama and roleplay
  - —by using their imaginations
  - —by expressing themselves creatively
  - —by teaching others
- the mix of persons in your group is different from that found in any other group;
- the length of the actual time you have for teaching in a session may vary from thirty minutes to ninety minutes;
- the physical place where your class meets is not exactly like the place where any other group or class meets;
- your teaching skills, experiences, and preferences are unlike anyone else's.

We encourage you to discover and develop the ways you can best use the information and learning ideas in this leader's guide with your particular class. To get started, we suggest you try following these steps:

1. Think and pray about your individual class members. Who are they? What are they like? Why are they involved in this particular Bible study class at this particular time in their lives? What seem to be their needs? How do you think they learn best?

2. Think and pray about your class members as a group. A group takes on a character that can be different from the particular characters of the individuals who make up that group. How do your class members interact? What do they enjoy doing together? What would help them become stronger as a group?

3. Keep in mind that you are teaching this class for the sake of the class members, in order to help them increase in their faithfulness as disciples of Jesus Christ. Teachers sometimes fall prey to the danger of teaching in ways that are easiest for themselves. The best teachers accept the discomfort of taking risks and stretching their teaching skills in order to focus on what will really help the class members learn and grow in their faith.

4. Read the chapter in the study book. Read the assigned Bible passages. Read the background Bible passages, if any. Work through the Dimension 1 questions in the study book. Make a list of any items you do not understand and need to research further using such tools as Bible dictionaries, concordances, Bible atlases, and commentaries. In

other words, do your homework. Be prepared with your own knowledge about the Bible passages being studied by your class.

5. Read the chapter's material in the leader's guide. You might want to begin with the "Additional Bible Helps," found at the *end* of each chapter in the leader's guide. Then look at each learning idea in the "Learning Menu."

6. Spend some time with the "Learning Menu." Notice that the "Learning Menu" is organized around Dimensions 1, 2, and 3 in the study book. Recognizing that different adults and adult classes will learn best using different teaching/learning methods, in each of the three dimensions you will find
   - —at least one learning idea that is primarily discussion-based;
   - —at least one learning idea that begins with a method other than discussion, but which may lead into discussion.

   Make notes about which learning ideas will work best given the unique makeup and setting of your class.

7. Decide on a lesson plan: Which learning ideas will you lead the class members through when? What materials will you need? What other preparations do you need to make? How long do you plan to spend on a particular learning idea?

8. Many experienced teachers have found that they do better if they plan more than they actually use during a class session. They also know that their class members may become frustrated if they try to do too much during a class session. In other words
   - —plan more than you can actually use. That way, you have back-up learning ideas in case something does not work well or something takes much less time than you thought.
   - —don't try to do everything listed in the "Learning Menu." We have intentionally offered you much more than you can use in one class session.
   - —be flexible while you teach. A good lesson plan is only guide for your use as you teach people. Keep the focus on your class members, not your lesson plan.

9. After you teach, evaluate the class session. What worked well? What did not? What did you learn from your experience of teaching that will help you plan for the next class session?

May God's Spirit be upon you as you lead your class on their *Journey Through the Bible*!

1

Luke
1:26–45

GOOD NEWS, BAD NEWS

LEARNING MENU

Keeping in mind the ways in which your class members learn best, as well as their needs and interests, choose at least one learning segment from each of the three Dimensions.

Dimension 1:
What Does the Bible Say?

Preferably, class members will read each chapter and answer the questions in Dimension 1 before the class session. However, some classes may wish to
● share and check their answers together during class;
● discuss their answers as part of the class session;
● work on answering the questions together during class.
Spend the least amount of time necessary in looking at the questions and answers in Dimension 1. Dimensions 2 and 3 contain the "meat" of the chapter's material. Dimension 1 is intended only to get you started with reading and thinking about the biblical text.
    Learning segments A, B, and C are designed to help

class members respond to Dimension 1 questions listed on pages 3-4 of the study book.

(A) Explore the connection between Luke and Acts.

Since this is the first lesson in the series about Luke, you may wish to spend a few minutes discussing the connection between Luke and Acts.
● Ask the students how they responded to the first question in Dimension 1, page 3 of the study book.
● Look at the sidebar, page 4 of the study book, with the quotations from Luke and Acts. If you wish to say more about "Theophilus," you may look at the Additional Bible Helps at the end of this lesson.
If you wish, you may move directly from this point to activity (E) under Dimension 2.

(B) Draw a timeline.

● Look at the second question. Expand it by asking the class to help you draw a timeline of the events described in Luke 1, listing the characters in the story and when they come in.
At the end, your timeline should look something like the following:

♦ Angel visits Zechariah
  ♦ Zechariah returns home
    ♦ Elizabeth pregnant
      ♦ Five months in seclusion
        ♦ Sixth month: Annunciation
          Visitation
          Song of Mary
        ♦ Ninth month: Mary returns
          Birth of John
        ♦ Prophecy of Zechariah
          ♦ Birth of Jesus (Luke 2)

(C) Read the passage.

- Read the first phrase of the passage (verse 26), "in the sixth month."
- Ask the class what this means. (Obviously, the answer is that this is the sixth month of Elizabeth's pregnancy; that story is to be found in the earlier verses of chapter 1.)

Dimension 2:
What Does the Bible Mean?

(D) Compare Luke/Acts with New Testament Letters.

If you chose activity (A) under Dimension 1, you may wish to move directly from that option to this one.

- Ask students to compare the thickness of Luke and Acts in the Bible with the thickness of the pages from Romans to Philemon (understood by many to be the Pauline letters.)
- Compare your findings with the sidebar in the study book, page 5.
- Ask the following questions:
—Are your findings surprising?
—If so, why do you find it surprising?

(E) Explore the context in which Luke wrote.

- If the students have read the material in their study books before coming to class, ask them to summarize some of the events that occurred between the resurrection of Jesus and the time Luke wrote.
—What were the risks and difficulties that Christians now faced?
- Make a list of responses and write them on newsprint. Keep this list for later use.
- If the class did not read the material before the session, read the paragraph that begins "Luke wrote his two books about the year A.D. 80."
- Ask the class to help you make a list similar to that described under activity (B).

(F) Explore the difficulty the Announcement brought to Mary.

- Point out that the episodes we are studying are usually called the "Annunciation" and the "Visitation." The study book suggests calling these events simply the "Announcement" and the "Visit."
- Discuss the questions:
—Does it make any difference what we call these events? (These names may have been more common in the past, when they were first used. We have not updated them, as we have updated much of the rest of our language.)
—Why do you think that so often in Bible study and in religious matters we use strange and uncommon words, rather than those that we use in everyday life? (We tend to use strange words, because that seems to preserve the majesty of the Bible and of our faith. It is easier to establish a distance between ourselves and what those words mean. Strange words challenge us less than everyday words.)

(G) Imagine that you are Mary.

- Ask class members to imagine that they are Mary. (Imagine they are all young women, single, in a society where premarital sex is considered a crime and often punished as such.)
- Ask them to imagine that someone comes and talks to them. (This person has no special appearance whereby you can know it is an angel. The notion that angels always appear in some sort of supernatural form is not necessarily biblical. In the Bible, sometimes people can tell that angels are special messengers and sometimes they cannot.)
- Read Luke 1:26-38, stopping at various points to ask the class how they react to the reading.
—How do you react when the angel tells you that you will have a child, even without being married?

(H) Consider your response to the Announcement.

- Instead of using activity (G), ask one of the members of the class to dramatize how they would respond to such an announcement. (If possible, talk with the class member before the class meets, so that this person will have some time to reflect and prepare.)

(I) Examine the political situtation.

- The study book material does not deal with the political situation in which Mary lived. You may wish to insert that element to show that the news the angel brought was difficult for Mary. Use the following material for a brief lecture.

What Was the Political Situation?

Mary was a Jewish woman living at a time when Israel was under Roman rule. For a long time, the Jewish people had been dreaming of the restoration of the throne of David, and for this reason there already had been a number of uprisings, some of which had been drowned in blood. (Shortly after the time of Jesus' birth, there would be one such uprising in Galilee, and there would be many dead.) Already at the time of the announcement of the birth, it was clear that there was rebellion in the air, and that the Roman authorities would do all that was in their power to suppress any attempt at rebellion.

The angel told Mary that the son she would bear would receive "the throne of his ancestor David," (32) and that "he will reign over the house of Jacob forever . . ." (33). These were words of sedition. If Mary had told anyone that she expected to have a son who would sit upon the throne of David, and the Roman authorities caught a whiff of it, she would not have had long to live!

Thus, the announcement of Gabriel was disturbing news, not only because it would pit Mary against the moral expectations of society and against the religious ethics of her people, but also because it would put her in a position of difficulty with the Roman Empire itself—she, a young woman from far away Galilee!

(J) Express Mary's thoughts.

- Invite class members to consider Mary's thoughts as she journeyed the distance between Nazareth and Elizabeth's home town in Judea.
- Instruct class members to close their eyes and imagine that they are young Mary. They have just received word that they will bear a child. What concerns or questions would they identify as they travel?
- When class members have had several moments of quiet reflection (perhaps 2-3 minutes), encourage them to form small groups of three to five and share the things Mary might have identified.
- Here are some concerns identified by the writer of this lesson:
—What will Elizabeth say when I tell her that I am also pregnant?
—Elizabeth and Zechariah are righteous, blameless people (Luke 1:6). Will Elizabeth and Zechariah refuse to take me in?
—Will they receive me, hoping to make me confess that I have sinned?
—Perhaps I should have stayed home!
(Apparently the distance between Nazareth and Eliza-

beth's town in Judea was considerable, and although Elizabeth was six months pregnant her family in Nazareth did not know it. Luke tells us that when Mary expressed her perplexity, Gabriel responded by pointing to Elizabeth. In so doing, Gabriel was offering Elizabeth to Mary as a source of strength and understanding.)

(K) Compare the women's situations.

- Divide a piece of newsprint into three columns, each with a heading: "Elizabeth," "Both," and "Mary."
- Ask the class to list the points that the two had in common, and write them in the middle column.
- Ask what made each of them different and write these contrasts in the appropriate columns, as in the following example.
- Ask the class to discuss how these similarities and differences would have helped them stand in solidarity and support of each other.

Elizabeth	Both	Mary
married	women	single
old	pregnant	young
happy	Jewish	worried
Judea		Galilee

Dimension 3:
What Does the Bible Mean to Us?

(L) Experience "good news/bad news."

- Ask the class if they know a "good news/bad news" joke.
- If you know one joke that would be appropriate, you may wish to tell it. (Here is one example. A farmer had a son who was given a horse. When people came to congratulate him, he said, "We shall see." Then the son fell from his horse and broke a leg. When people came to express their sorrow, he said, "We shall see." Then there was a war, the army came to carry all able-bodied youths to war, and the farmer's son, who had a broken leg, was spared. When people came to congratulate him, he said "We shall see." The story goes on and on. The point is that what seems bad news is good news, and vice versa.)
- Say that, in a way, the Gospel of Luke is a bad news/good news story. The coming of Jesus is good news; but not everyone can receive him as such. Indeed, in the course of our study we shall find many who did not find Jesus to be "good news." Can the class name some of them? (This group would include Pharisees,

religious and self-righteous people in general, some of the rich, and so forth.) During the rest of these sessions be on the lookout for persons who did not understand Jesus to be "good news." In the announcement of the birth of Jesus, some of what the angel said would be good news for Mary, and some would be bad news.

● Explore the story of the two students preparing for ordained ministry, shared on page 8 of the leader's guide.

—Is the call of God good news to both of them?

—In what sense?

(M) Discuss conditions that make it hard to hear the good news.

● Remind the class of the particularly trying times in which Luke wrote his Gospel. (It was because of those times that he wrote his story showing that the good news of the Gospel stands even in the midst of all sorts of bad news. Christians were persecuted; they were exiled; they were ridiculed. Still their message was good news!)

● Discuss the following questions:

—What are some conditions in our society today that make it difficult to hear the good news?

—Is it easier to be a Christian today than in Luke's time? Why? Why not?

—In the Gospel of Luke, many of the Pharisees heard the preaching of Jesus as bad news—or, what is the same— as good news that was not for them. Is it conceivable that someone today will hear the good news of the Gospel as bad news? Can you give some examples?

(N) Explore potential support in the church.

● Discuss:

—There is a song that says, quite tongue-in-cheek, that "I can be a Christian by myself." Why is this a false statement?

—What are some areas of the Christian life in which some of us find that we need the support of others?

(O) Simulate the support of the church.

● If time allows, choose two volunteers.

● Invite one to sit on a chair in the middle of the room. Forbid him or her to get up.

● Blindfold the second volunteer.

● Take three books of three different colors, place them in different parts of the room, and ask each volunteer to collect all three books and place them on the table in a certain order (for instance, the blue book on top and the black one at the bottom). Obviously, they cannot do it.

● Then ask the volunteers to do the assignment together. (The person seated can give directions to the one who is blindfolded. The task is not difficult when done cooperatively.)

● Ask the class what can be learned from the simulation. (We each have gifts and limitations. If we try to "go it alone," we shall certainly fail. In solidarity and cooperation we can succeed where individually we would fail.)

● Ask class members to give examples of how Christians support each other by bringing to bear a variety of gifts. (You may draw examples from the class itself, from the congregation, or even from the worldwide church, where various congregations bring together different gifts to carry forth the mission. You may also wish to refer to Paul's famous passage in 1 Corinthians 12:12-27, where he compares the church to a body in which various members work together for the benefit of all.)

(P) Covenant together.

● Invite class members to formally commit to study the Gospel of Luke together, to help each other understand more deeply what the Gospel means, and to attend and participate in as many sessions as possible, even when other options might seem more interesting or exciting.

(Q) Worship.

● End the study session with a prayer of thanksgiving for the Gospel and for each other.

Additional Bible Helps

Theophilus

The identity of Theophilus is uncertain, although Luke dedicated his two books to him. The name was rather common, not only among Gentiles, but also among Jews. To complicate matters, the name itself means "lover of God" or "beloved of God." Therefore, some have suggested that "Theophilus" was nobody in particular, but was simply the name Luke gave to his readers, whoever they might be.

Most scholars, however, reject this theory, mostly because Luke addressed this particular Theophilus as "most excellent," employing a word that was normally reserved for aristocratic Romans of equestrian rank—that is, the rank immediately below the senatorial. Since in the rest of his two-volume work Luke was very careful with his titles, this would seem to indicate that his Theophilus was indeed an aristocratic Roman who had "been instructed" in the Christian faith (Luke 1:4).

Elizabeth, Mary, and the Theme of the "Barren Woman"

One theme that we have chosen not to highlight in our

study of this passage, but which would have been obvious to any reader in the first century who had been steeped in the Hebrew Scriptures, is that of the barren woman who conceived by divine intervention.

The background of this theme is obviously a society in which fertility was considered of great importance, for it was what made a people great. It was also a society in which infertility was usually considered to be the woman's fault, rather than her mate's. In such a society, "barrenness" appeared as a curse, and the act of conceiving as a blessing and, in the case of the woman who was thought to be barren, even as a vindication.

This theme has already appeared in the Book of Genesis. The story of Abraham and Sarah is well known. Sarah was barren until God intervened (Genesis 16:1 and 17:15-21). Later, their son Isaac was married to Rebekah, and "Isaac prayed to the Lord for his wife, because she was barren; and the Lord granted his prayer, and his wife Rebekah conceived" (Genesis 25:21). Finally, in Genesis 30 we have a heart-rending story of how Rachel felt unloved by Jacob, because he had children from her sister Leah and from their two servants, but not from her. Eventually, at the end of that chapter, we are told that "God remembered Rachel, and God heeded her and opened her womb" (22).

Later, in 1 Samuel, we have the case of Hannah, who was married to Elkanah. Elkanah's other wife, Peninnah, gave him other sons, and even mocked Hannah for her barrenness. Eventually Hannah, through God's intervention, delivered the great prophet Samuel.

There are many other stories of barrenness in the Old Testament—to the point that when the prophet wishes to announce tidings of great joy he says: "Sing, O barren one who did not bear; burst into song and shout, you who have not been in labor!" (Isaiah 54:1)

All this would have been known to a reader in the first century, for it was a relatively common theme in Bible commentary and study. When coming upon the story of Elizabeth, such a reader would not have been surprised. Here is one more case of a barren woman who conceived.

The new twist would be in the story of Mary, which becomes entwined with that of Elizabeth. In a way Mary, being a virgin, is the barren woman par excellence.

Early Christian readers would have seen in this the culmination and fulfillment of a pattern: God intervenes where there seems to be no possibility, and creates something unexpected. To such readers, it would have been significant that, after Elizabeth and Mary, the theme of the barren woman disappeared—as if it had already been played out.

Why did Luke begin his Gospel with these stories of barren women? Several reasons have been suggested; most probably, he did so because he was closing the book on the story of women as being merely somebody's mother or somebody's wife. From this point on, as you will have ample opportunity to see in your journey through Luke and Acts, women will appear as persons in their own right—as disciples, as financial supporters of the mission, as teachers, as leaders in the church, and so forth.

The Song of Mary
Since in this volume of *Journey Through the Bible* we must center our attention on selected passages, we shall not be able to study the song of Mary, which follows immediately after the passage we are studying (Luke 1:46-55). This song is usually called the *Magnificat*, which is the Latin word with which the traditional Latin translation begins.

You may wish to compare it with the song (or prayer) of Hannah in 1 Samuel 2:1-10. This was Hannah's response when she finally conceived and bore Samuel, and was then able to consecrate him to the Lord. It was clearly a song of vindication, where Hannah praised God for having vindicated her by giving her a son.

The fact that Luke included the song of Mary, so clearly patterned after Hannah's, is a further indication that the stories of Elizabeth and Mary should be read in the context of the general theme of the barren woman.

A STUDY IN CONTRASTS

2

Luke 2:1-20

LEARNING MENU

Keep in mind the ways in which your class members learn best as you choose one or more teaching methods from Dimensions 1, 2, and 3.

Dimension 1:
What Does the Bible Say?

(A) Read the text.

Read aloud the Bible passage, Luke 2:1-20.

(B) Discuss how events are dated.

You may wish to begin the session with a discussion about how events are dated. See the sidebar on this page.

(C) Examine the story of the shepherds.

- Ask the class to list their responses to the third question in the study book, page 12.
- Now ask them to explain why they gave those responses. (Doing this will focus attention on the story of the shep-

---

Dating Events

Today when we say "A.D. 1987," everyone knows what we mean. In ancient times, people dated events from a variety of other events. Some used the founding of the city of Rome and would say that something happened in the year 600 *ab urbe condita*—"from the founding of the city." Others would choose events that were particularly known to their audience.

Writing to an audience in the first century, probably in the vicinity of the city of Antioch in Syria, Luke dated his story on the basis of the reign of Augustus and the governorship of Quirinius in Syria. His readers thereby attained an approximate idea of the time he meant.

Note that Luke gave the matter an interesting twist: the passage begins ". . . in those days" (1). The days to which he referred are those of which he spoke in the first chapter: the time of the pregnancies of Elizabeth and Mary. In other words, Luke reversed the expected procedure. Instead of dating the events in the hill country of Judea by the events in Rome, he dated the events in Rome on the basis of what was happening in the hill country!

8

herds, and how they react and act at various points in the story.)

(D) Identify the characters.

- Ask the class to make a list of the characters that should be included in a play based on this passage. If no one mentions them, make certain that Augustus and Quirinius are included in the list.
- Suggest that the play will take place on a double stage with the stories of Mary and Joseph, the shepherds, and angels on one stage, and Augustus and Quirinius on the other.
- Discuss:
—What would you have Augustus and/or Quirinius do and say while the rest of the play is unfolding on the other stage?
- In order to facilitate this process, you may wish to share with the class some of the material that appears later on under the heading Additional Bible Helps.

Dimension 2:
What Does the Bible Mean?

(E) Study the map.

- Using the map in the study book (inside back cover), ask the class to look quickly at the passage for last week as well as the one for this week, and imagine that Luke is a TV cameraman.
- Discuss:
—Where does he "zoom in" on a small place?
—Where does he "zoom out" to the larger picture?
- Remind the class of the smallness of Bethlehem, as attested both in Micah 5:2 and in the text of the carol, "O Little Town of Bethlehem."
- Contrast this picture with the vastness of the Roman Empire. (If the class seems to enjoy this manner of understanding a literary piece, you may wish to carry the cinematographic analogy further, and have them discuss the camera technique of the first two chapters of Luke. Note that the first scene takes place at the Temple, where Zechariah is offering incense. We follow him to his home, where Elizabeth conceives. Next the camera shifts to Nazareth and focuses on the angel and Mary, whom it then follows to Elizabeth's home and back to Nazareth. Having left Mary at Nazareth, the scene returns to the home of Elizabeth and Zechariah, for the birth of John the Baptist. Then, at the beginning of chapter 2, the camera briefly zooms out to encompass the entire Roman Empire, and immediately focuses again on Mary. After the birth, an element of surprise is introduced when the camera turns to some previously

unmentioned shepherds. In the end these shepherds bring us back to the manger.)

(F) Center your attention on the census.

According to the law, the census bureau must count all the population of the United States every ten years. Yet, experts tell us that at the end of every census there is always a significant undercount. This undercount takes place mostly in poor neighborhoods, where for various reasons people do not wish to be counted. This happens in spite of all the assurances the census bureau gives to the effect that its data will be used for no other purpose.

If that is the case in our society, where there is quite a flow of information and rights of appeal, can you imagine what it would have been like in the Roman Empire, when the emperor ordered a census? This is the context in which the Nativity story takes place, but a context that we often neglect.

In order to make this point, you may choose one of the following options:
- Share with the class some of the information about census taking and taxation that appears in the section on Additional Bible Helps.
- Ask the class to try to imagine what people thought about the census that was taking place. Lead the class in a discussion on this topic. (Make certain that the feelings of anxiety and anger that must have been part of the common reaction to the census come out in such discussion.)
- Divide the class into two groups.
—One group is to be the people at the inn, who have come to Bethlehem in order to be registered.
—The second group is to be the shepherds, guarding their flock at night.
- Ask each group to imagine what the conversation was about that night, while the census was being taken, and to prepare a brief skit (no more than two or three minutes each) expressing the gist of that conversation.

(G) Discuss "Why Bethlehem?"

- Discuss question 2 raised in the study book, page 12.
- Enrich the discussion of class members by sharing the information provided in the box after class members have shared their insights:

Why Bethlehem?

Luke told us that Joseph had to go to Bethlehem "because he was descended from the house and family of David" (4). The edict issued by Augustus ordered that all had to go to the city of their ancestors in order to be registered. From the point of view of the Roman authorities, this was a way (1) to prevent fraud and (2) to keep track of families and nations. Since much of taxation and government took place through national and regional units, it was important for the government to know who belonged to what group.

For Joseph, this was a most inconvenient trip, which had to be undertaken precisely when Mary was about to give birth, and on which he had no choice. Here another of Luke's magnificent contrasts comes into play: Joseph was a descendant of King David, yet he had to go to Bethlehem, the city of that great king, at the command of Emperor Augustus.

When he arrived at the city of his ancestors, he who was of royal lineage found that there was no room at the inn! Thus, part of the contrast that Luke was drawing was between a foreign "Johnny-come-lately" king and an ancient royal family, which was dispossessed to the point that its child had to be laid in a manger, because there was no room in the inn.

Athanasius (bishop of Alexandria in the fourth century) used a similar contrast to underscore the significance of the Incarnation (Christ's coming in the flesh). "When a great king enters a large city and lives in one of its houses, the entire city is honored. . . . The entire city receives special treatment, because the king has established his residence in one of its houses. The same is true with the Monarch of all. He has come into our own, and taken up residence in one like us. Therefore the entire conspiracy of the enemy against us is stopped, and the corruption of death is destroyed. For our entire human race was ruined, and the Lord and Savior of all, God's own Son, came to join us and thus to be the end of death. (*On the Incarnation of the Word of God*, 9.)

(H) Read the shepherds and the angels passage (Luke 2: 8-21).

- Ask the "shepherds" in your class, those who played such roles in learning segment (F), to react to each stage in the narrative.
- Read verses 8 and 9.
- Discuss:
—Why are you terrified? (A helpful procedure would be to place the story in a modern setting where people would be equally terrified if someone came to them suddenly at night. Think, for instance, of one of the many countries in the world where people have reason

to fear the forces of national security, or of one of the other countries where people have to fear bandits and rebels. Palestine in the first century was probably both. These shepherds were talking among themselves, thinking that no one could overhear. Suddenly someone appeared before them, and there was a great light! If this were to happen to us in the countryside of Guatemala or Peru, we certainly would be terrified!)
- Read verses 10-12.
- Discuss:
—What reason did the angel give why they should not be afraid? (The angel did not simply command them to be joyful. He gave them a reason for joy: "good news . . . for all the people.")
- Remind the class of the subject of our last study: "Good News/Bad News."
- Discuss:
—Suppose you were a shepherd, in the circumstances we have been studying. Would this really be good news to you?
—If it was true that the Messiah had been born, would this not disrupt your life? (Certainly. The coming of the Messiah could easily cause more strife and bring about even worse forms of Roman repression.)
- Read verses 12-14.
- Note the word *sign* in verse 12. (In most of the New Testament, a "sign" was a miracle of importance, something so extraordinary that it proclaimed the power and authority of Jesus. Not so in Luke, where Jesus consistently refused to offer such "signs" (see, for instance, Luke 11:16, 29-32). Later this week, in one of the readings included in the Daily Bible Journey Plan, we shall be told that Jesus will be "a sign that will be opposed" (Luke 2:34). Here, in Luke 2:12, the "sign" that the shepherds were offered was not some miraculous event, or a great light, but only that they "will find a child wrapped in bands of cloth and lying in a manger." After the overwhelming experience of the angel's message and the celestial choir, all they would find would be a baby in a manger! Once again, Luke points to the contrast between what we would expect of God and how God really acts.)
- Finally, read verses 15-20.
- Discuss:
—Was the shepherd's attitude one of mere curiosity? (That may have been the case at the beginning. By the end of the passage, however, that certainly was no longer the case. The shepherds glorified and praised God, and those who heard them were amazed. Note again the unexpected twist of the story. We are not told, as we would expect, that it was the angelic choir that most amazed them. After hearing the choir, all they did was go look. It was after seeing this babe in a manger that they began to tell what they had heard and seen, and to glorify and praise God.)

As you introduce this section, remember to build on what was said last week about the relationship between good news and bad news. The good news of the gospel may seem bad news for those who have much to give up and would rather not. The reverse is also true. Those whose life is full of bad news are often more ready to hear and heed the good news of the gospel.

Remember also that this passage, so well known to us as the basis for so many Christmas pageants, is a study in contrasts. One of the contrasts that Luke established in this passage, and throughout his Gospel, was the contrast between the powerful and secure, who acted as if they had no need for God, and those who, for whatever reason, were open to God's action. Augustus on his throne issued edicts and had little need to listen to anyone, let alone God. Quirinius implemented Augustus' decrees, and as such was a powerful man. Yet it was not to Augustus nor to Quirinius, not to Rome nor to Antioch, that God came. It was to a manger, and to some shepherds guarding their flocks at night in a remote corner of the Empire.

(I) Examine our need to change perspective.

● Remind the class members that the study book encourages us to change our perspective. To do this, tell them that one of the best books ever written about St. Francis refers to him as "God's juggler." The reason for this is that in Francis' times jugglers would stand on their heads as they performed their acts. What this author claims is that Francis was who he was because he saw the world upside down. For his father and his friends, success was to make money. For Francis, success was to give away money. For the bishop and the rulers of his town, success was to rule over others. For Francis, success was to be everybody's brother and to serve all.
● Ask the question:
—Is that what Luke is all about?
—Is he trying to see the world upside down, where the powerful and the rich are not as fortunate as they think, and where the seemingly secure are in fact the closest to destruction?
● Lead the class in a discussion. (If there is resistance to such an understanding of the Gospel, do not force agreement. Rather, leave the matter open, to be answered in the rest of our study of Luke.)

(J) Consider a definition for success.

● Read the first of the three questions that appear on page 18 of the study book.

● Ask the class to think for a moment about what they would consider success.
● Discuss two points:
—What would Luke say about our understandings of success?
—Are we organizing our lives in order to achieve the sort of success that we have described, or another?

(K) Write your epitaph.

● Distribute pencils and paper.
● Ask each member of the class to write privately, on the basis of their understanding of success, the epitaph that they would like to see inscribed on their tombstone.
● Tell students not to share their epitaph with anyone, but to carry it with them, and read it again each day during the coming week as they continue their journey through the Bible.
● Suggest that at that time they ask themselves if they are really living with that goal in mind.

(L) Consider how you want your church to look.

● Read questions 2 and 3 on page 18 of the study book.
● Ask the class how they would respond to those questions.
● Pose the question:
—On the basis of this discussion, how do we want our church to look?
—What can we do to bring it to that point?

Augustus
Augustus, whose original name was Gaius Octavius, was adopted as a son by Julius Caesar, who also made him his heir. When, after Caesar's death, Octavius learned that he was the great man's heir, he changed his name to Gaius Julius Caesar Octavianus. The name "Augustus" is in fact a title, meaning something between "reverend" and "divine." It was granted to him by the Roman Senate in the year 27 B.C., when he offered to give up his power. Instead, the Senate gave him even greater powers and honors, including the title of "Augustus." Although eventually this title was given to all emperors, when used as a name (as Luke used it), it refers to this first and most distinguished of emperors.

Augustus was neither a tyrant nor a model of a man. He attained his power through a series of armed struggles and bloody feats, including the death of three hundred senators. Yet he was respected for his insistence of the rule of law, for his sense of fairness, and for the glory that the Empire attained under him. He died in A.D. 19 and was succeeded by his son-in-law Tiberius, who was emperor at the time of the Crucifixion.

Quirinius

From the point of view of Roman history, Quirinius is of much less importance. However, he has been much discussed by scholars of the New Testament, for there are difficulties reconciling what Luke tells us here with what is known from other sources. We know for certain that Quirinius was governor of Syria beginning in the year A.D. 6. According to Jewish historian Josephus, there was a census in Palestine at about that time. But this was long after the death of King Herod (4 B.C.). Scholars have suggested several solutions to the puzzle:

- Luke simply created the story of the census in order to bring the Holy Family to Bethlehem. The main difficulty with that theory is that a public event such as a census would still be remembered by people living at the time of Luke's writing, who would immediately recognize the inaccuracy.
- Quirinius, whose earlier career was not completely clear, was governor of Syria more than once (perhaps the first time as an associate to another governor).
- The phrase translated as "the first registration taken while Quirinius was governor" (2) should be interpreted as "the registration that took place before Quirinius." In that case, it would be a census different from the one recorded by Josephus.

Although it is impossible to determine the exact date of this particular census, much is known about the manner in which a census was taken in the Roman Empire. Julius Caesar was the first to order that such a thing be done. This was to list, not only inhabitants, but also real estate and movable assets, such as herds of animals. That first census took twenty-five years to complete! By then, it was obviously out-of-date. Therefore, in the early Empire the census was updated every five years (later every fifteen years).

The main purpose of a census was to determine what could be levied from each province in the form of taxes and of soldiers for auxiliary troops. Since in ancient Rome citizens were free of taxes, the Roman Empire never developed the notion that taxes were something that the governed pay in exchange for the benefits of government. On the contrary, taxes were a tribute paid by the conquered to the conquerors (the Latin word for what we today would call "taxes" was *tributum*). Apart from minor taxes on inheritance and some forms of trade, there were two main taxes: the land tax and the head tax. The land tax was not based simply on acreage, but also on the productive capability of the land. The head tax tried to take into account the economic status and productivity of each person. The main purpose of a census was then to determine how many "heads" and how many units for land taxation each region had.

The Roman Empire never had a budget. As the need arose, quotas were assigned to each province and region. The rights to collect such quotas were then sold to tax farmers or "publicans," whose profit was mainly in the difference between the quota that the government expected and the taxes they actually collected.

In Judea, under Julius Caesar, cereal crops were taxed at the rate of twenty-five percent. But the farmer was responsible for transporting that fourth of his crop to the places of collection, often long distances away. Given the high cost of cartage in ancient times, the burden was considerable. To this had to be added municipal and local taxes exacted by government and religious authorities. In Judea, this included the annual half shekel that all Jews had to pay to the Temple, as well as the traditional tithe and other offerings prescribed by the law of Moses.

Finally, since this story is set in the time of Herod the Great, you may also wish to know that Herod himself was one of the richest persons in the Roman Empire. Eventually a delegation of Jewish notables was sent to Rome to protest Herod's exactions and his ruthless and corrupt methods of collecting taxes. If this was the feeling of the Jewish aristocracy, it is not difficult to imagine how poorer Jews (including the shepherds of whom Luke speaks) must have felt.

3

$\mathcal{F}$ROM PREACHING TO MEDDLING

Luke 4:16-30

LEARNING MENU

Keeping in mind the ways in which your class members learn best as well as their needs and interests, choose at least one learning segment from each of the three Dimensions.

Dimension 1:
What Does the Bible Say?

Your purpose in this first dimension of the lesson is basically to whet the students' appetite for the lesson. You also want to get them to read the text as a whole and as part of the entire Gospel of Luke. While the dimensions presented will help students grapple with the questions asked of them in the study book, you may wish to invite students to share their answers to the questions on pages 19-20 of the study book in small groups as members arrive and before the actual session begins.

(A) Read the text.

Invite members of the class to read Luke 4:16-30 aloud.

(B) Study the map.

Use the map from the inside back cover of the study book. You will also need to refer to your Bible.

● Invite the class to locate various places on the map referred to by the text.

—Verse 16 of the text uses the phrase, "he came to Nazareth." Locate the city of Nazareth on the map. (Nazareth is a town in lower Galilee.)

—Jesus traveled to Nazareth. Where was he coming from? (If we read the earlier verses of the same chapter, all that we are told is that, after being tempted in the desert, Jesus returned to Galilee, and that he began to teach in the surrounding country. In verse 23 Jesus declared that he expected people in Nazareth to ask him to do what he had done in Capernaum, a city in Galilee that Luke did not mention until 4:31, immediately after this passage. Did Luke make a mistake? Probably not. Rather, he took for granted that Capernaum was one of the cities in Galilee that Jesus had visited before coming to Nazareth, and it was only after telling about the episode in Nazareth that Luke took the time to explain what it was that Jesus had done in Capernaum.)

—Locate Galilee and the city of Capernaum on the map.

(C) Consider Jesus' reference to Isaiah.

Not everyone in your class will know that Jesus quoted from Isaiah during this incident recorded in Luke. Jesus applied Isaiah's words to himself.

- Ask:
- —Did you realize that it was as a result of this sermon that the people in Nazareth tried to kill Jesus?
- —Why is it that when we read Scripture, we often leave out part of a story? (In this particular case, it is clear that the story did not end with Jesus reading from Isaiah and all the congregation being amazed at his teaching. On the contrary, it went on to a rather unpleasant development with the folk from his own town wishing to kill Jesus.)

It is not necessary to come to a consensus in this discussion. You are simply alerting the class to the ease with which we ignore part of a biblical text, while giving great importance to the rest.

(D) Study Old Testament passages.

- Ask three members of the class to read beforehand the three main passages in the Old Testament to which this passage refers: Isaiah 61:1-3; 1 Kings 17:8-24; and 2 Kings 5. Encourage these members to research further information through Bible commentaries available in your church or public library or pastor's study. Some information may be gathered in the Additional Bible Helps section of the leader's guide.
- As you read the passage in class, interrupt your reading at appropriate points to give these three persons an opportunity to tell what they have learned. Have a large wall map available so that class members reporting can point out the location of Zarephath and other places. This will help clarify the meaning of the text. In any case, we shall be using these three references in the next dimension of our study. (Since these stories are so crucial to an understanding of the text in Luke, we shall return to them in the next dimension. Therefore, before deciding whether to use this option and how, look at the options under Dimension 2.)

Dimension 2:
What Does the Bible Mean?

The passage we are studying has a clear dividing point, or a radical change in the middle of it. At first people were quite positive toward what Jesus was saying. Then they turned against him to the point that they tried to kill him. To understand the passage, it is necessary to understand both what Jesus was saying at the beginning and what he said that made people turn against him. Therefore, as you choose options for presenting this dimension, make sure that the options you select will help the class understand both elements in the text.

(E) Consider your reactions.

- Ask the class the following questions:
- —Suppose that you were Jews, living in a rather impoverished and exploited area in the first century. Then someone told you that "this Scripture had been fulfilled in your hearing" (21). What would you think?
- —Suppose further, that the preacher was someone from your own hometown, who had been away for a while and had gained some fame for his teaching and his miracles. How do you think you would react?

(Apparently, the people in Nazareth reacted quite positively. We have no indication that they disliked what Jesus had to say until the end of verse 22. On the contrary, they were "amazed at the gracious words that came from his mouth".)

- Make certain, before you move to another point, that the class is quite clear that the reason why the people in Nazareth reacted negatively to Jesus' sermon was not that he claimed that in his ministry the prophecies were being fulfilled. That may be the case in other instances, but not here. In Luke they liked Jesus' sermon, even when he said that the prophecies were being fulfilled. On the contrary, they were probably quite happy that something as important as this event was happening in their often despised town. (Remember the words of Nathanael in John 1:46.)

(F) Consider our reactions further.

- Choose two or three people from the class and ask them to stand by the chalkboard or newsprint while you read and discuss the text.
- Ask them to imagine that they are part of this congregation in Nazareth.
- Using the map explain that Galilee in general, and Nazareth in particular, were not considered to be very important nor very religious by the Jews in Jerusalem. The Jews of Nazareth attempted to live as Jews in a setting strongly influenced by Gentiles.
- Invite class members standing by the chalkboard or newsprint to draw a smiling face each time they hear something from the text they like; ask them to draw a sad face each time they hear something in the text that they dislike or that saddens them.
- Read the text aloud, giving "artists" time to draw. Stop at the end of verse 22. Hopefully, you will have a predominance of happy faces.
- Invite those who drew faces to tell the class why they responded as they did.
- —How would other class members have responded? Any differently?

The first part of Jesus' sermon was fairly well received, even though Luke did not tell us much about what he said. The second part of the text is where listeners turned against Jesus (verses 23-30).

(G) Consider what angered the crowds.

- Read verses 23-24 aloud.
- Explain to the class the following points:
—Nazareth was far from "the center of the action." Citizens of Nazareth were happy because one of their own had become quite a teacher and because even miracles had been reported about him. Finally they felt they would be the center of things!
—Jesus told them that this idea was not so. He refused to perform in his own hometown any of the things that they had heard he had done elsewhere.
- Ask the class:
—If you had been part of that town and that congregation, how do you think you would have felt?
- Read verses 25.
- Point to Zarephath on the map. (It was even farther from Jerusalem than Galilee. It was Gentile territory.)
- Ask again:
—If you were part of that congregation, how would you feel?
- Read verse 27.
- Again, point to the map. (Syria was even farther away! It was not only a Gentile country; it was also enemy territory! Furthermore, shortly before the time of Jesus, Syria had been the great enemy against whom the Maccabees had fought.)
- Ask again:
—Now, as people in that congregation, how do you think you would feel?
- Finally, read verses 28-30 aloud.
- Ask the class why they think the people in Nazareth were so angry they wanted to kill Jesus.

(H) Discover the feelings of the congregation.

- Invite the same "artists" to return to the chalkboard or newsprint.
- Make it clear that verse 25 is a turning point in the story. Ask the "artists" to be very attentive to the change that takes place.
- Read aloud verses 23-24. (If the people in Nazareth were expecting Jesus to perform a miracle for them, he flatly refused.)
- Give the "artists" time to draw.
- Read aloud verses 25-26.
- Briefly tell the story of the widow of Zarephath. Underscore the fact that she was in faraway Zarephath of Sidon. (Refer, once again, to the map.)
- Finally, read verse 27.

- Tell the story of Naaman. (Make it clear, on the basis of the map, that Syria was even farther away. Furthermore, it was one of Israel's bitterest enemies.)
- Give the "artists" time to react. In all likelihood, you will now have an array of sad, puzzled, and angry faces.
- Invite "artists" to explain why they drew as they did.
- Ask the class to describe what they think the Nazareth congregation experienced and felt?
- End this part of the session by asking the class the following question:
—Do you understand now why the people in that congregation wanted to kill Jesus?

Optional Method:
- Prepare a few Bible questions and a prize beforehand. (Neither should be too elaborate. The questions should be fairly simple, and the prize may be no more than a piece of candy.)
- Announce that you are going to play a game in which simple Bible questions will be asked.
- Put the prize on the table so that everyone can see it.
- Begin asking your questions. As each question is answered, ask the person who answered it to move to one side of the room. (The class may begin to think that this is the favored side of the room.)
- Keep asking questions until several people stand on the "favored" side of the room.
- Announce that the prize is to be awarded to _____ and choose someone from the less favorable side of the room.
- Invite class members to share their reactions. (Reactions may include a mixture of shock, puzzlement, disappointment, and anger.)
- Use class reactions to help the class appreciate the way the congregation at Nazareth reacted to Jesus.
—What reasons did they have to expect that they were on the favored side?
—How did Jesus' sermon challenge those assumptions?

Dimension 3: What Does the Bible Mean to Us?

(I) Consider faith.

In the study book material, it is said that there is a sense in which faith should provide security, but that Luke's Gospel also emphasized the other side of the coin. A faith in which you can be too secure is not faith in the God of Israel and of Jesus. It is rather a form of idolatry. It is important that both sides of this coin be emphasized.
- Write on the chalkboard or newsprint, at the very top, the words "Christians can presume on God's favor."
- Below that heading, make two columns. Head one with the word *Yes*, the other with *No*.

- Ask the class to name reasons to answer "yes" and for reasons to answer "no."
- Make a list of abbreviated answers as the discussion progresses. (Obviously, the purpose is not to decide which of the two is the correct answer, but rather to point out the dangers of too simple an answer. As Christians, we must trust in God's love. Yet, we must not trust in that love as a means to special privilege or as a means to expect God to do whatever we please. Make this clear at the end of the discussion by pointing out that any answer or attitude that ignores the other side of the coin is incomplete.)

(J) Compose a map.

- Copy on the chalkboard the map that appears on the inside back cover. (Copy only the general outline without regional names.)
- In the place where the word "Jerusalem" would normally appear, write the word "Jesus."
- Near Jerusalem, write "apostles" and "saints."
- Where "Galilee" normally would appear, write "Us." You now have a sort of "spiritual map" of ourselves and the church.
- Ask the class for suggestions as to what to write in the places farther out where the original map says Zarephath and Syria.
—Whom do we consider to be further away from God and from Jesus than we are?
—How does it feel to be at this particular place in the spiritual map, neither entirely in nor entirely out?
—Do we wish we were holier?
—If so, is it because we think that would make us more secure of God's favor?
—Do we envy those "farther out," who get to do as they please?
—Do we resent them?
—Do we feel superior to them?
—What would we say if someone told us that God would show special favor toward one of them?
When we read the story in Luke, we drew angry faces every time Jesus said something that we thought the congregation in Nazareth would not like.
—Can we imagine some things that Jesus might say to us, on the basis of this "spiritual map" that might make us equally angry?
- List the responses on newsprint.
- Ask the question:
—Do you think that, were Jesus to come to us right here and now, he might say some of these things?
If the result of the discussion warrants it, you may wish to distribute pencils and paper and to ask each member of the class to write down the possible words of Jesus to our group and our situation that we would find most disturbing, possibly because they are true. Ask each person to put this piece of paper in his or her Bible and to look at it periodically as we continue our study of Luke.

Additional Bible Helps

The Year of Jubilee
A phrase in the quote from Isaiah that may not be altogether clear is "the year of the Lord's favor." Most scholars agree that the reference in Isaiah is to the ancient law of the "Year of Jubilee." According to Leviticus 25, this was to take place every fiftieth year, or after "seven weeks of years" (7 x 7 = 49). At that time, the law said, "you shall proclaim liberty throughout the land to all its inhabitants," and "you shall return, every one of you, to your property" (Leviticus 25:10-13).

What the first of these provisions meant was that, if any Jew had become a slave of another, such enslavement should be cancelled on the Jubilee Year.

The second provision was similar, but had to do with the land. According to the law, the land did not really belong to humans, but rather to God. This was the reason why it should not be abused. There were laws ordering that it be allowed to rest. That was also the reason why, strictly speaking, it could not be sold. "The land shall not be sold in perpetuity, for the land is mine; with me you are but aliens and tenants" (Leviticus 25:23). Thus, according to the law, when a piece of land was sold, this was only until the next Jubilee, when it would be returned to the original owner. (You may wish to read the entire chapter of Leviticus 25 to see how this was supposed to work.)

Whether the Jubilee Year was ever carried out in practice, and if so for how long, is much debated among scholars. In any case, the passage in Isaiah 61 that Jesus quoted clearly refers to the Year of Jubilee, and sees it as something that has not occurred in a long time, and for which the people long. This is true, not only of the phrase itself, "the year of the Lord's favor," but also of the rest of the passage, where phrases such as "release to the captives" and "good news to the poor" are to be understood in the context of the Jubilee. Both Isaiah and Jesus lived in times when there was much suffering because of unequal distribution of land and wealth. What both Isaiah and Jesus announced is a time when the justice envisioned in Leviticus would actually take place.

The Significance of Galilee
One of the most original and enlightening books regarding Galilee and its significance for understanding the Gospel is Virgilio Elizondo's *Galilean Journey: The Mexican-American Promise* (Orbis, 1984; page 51). In this book you may find very good descriptions of the situation of Galilee in the first century and how Galileans were regarded by the better Jews.

At the time of Jesus, Galilee was peopled by Phoenicians, Syrians, Arabs, Greeks, Orientals, and Jews. In this mixed, commerce-oriented society, some Jews had allowed their Jewish exclusivism to weaken, but others became more militantly exclusivist. . . . The Galilean Jews were regarded with patronizing contempt by the "pure minded" Jews of Jerusalem. The natural *mestizaje* (a Spanish word meaning a mixing of races and cultures) of Galilee was a sign of impurity and a cause for rejection. The Pharisees looked down upon "the people of the land" because they were ignorant of the law. The Sadducees looked down upon them because they were somewhat lax in matters of religious attendance and familiarity with the rules of Temple worship.

Elizondo then draws a parallel between Galilee and the experience of the Mexican-American, who also lives in and between two cultures and traditions; and he claims that examining this parallel can lead to a new and fruitful understanding of the Gospel. If your study group includes people whose experience is similar to what Elizondo describes, you will profit from reading his book. At the same time, it is important to remember that, while it is true that in the Gospels the Galileans generally received Jesus better than other Jews did, in this case they did not. When Jesus told them that God had shown favor to others who were even more marginal than they, they became so angry they were ready to kill him.

Sidon and Syria

Finally, you may wish to learn more about both Sidon and Syria. Look up these entries in a good dictionary of the Bible. You will learn that Sidon was a prosperous Phoenician city. Because it was near the borders of Israel (near the lands of the tribe of Asher), it was often seen by the people of Israel as a proud and dangerous neighbor. If you look up "Sidon" in a Bible concordance, you will find that the prophets repeatedly spoke against it and also announced its destruction. Also, you may take note that, according to Luke 6:17, Jesus later preached to people from Sidon. (According to Matthew 15:21 and Mark 7:31, Jesus actually went to Sidon; but Luke does not say so.)

Syria was the name that the Greek translation of the Old Testament (the "Septuagint") gave to the land of Aram. Therefore, you will find information on this subject under the headings of both "Syria" and "Aram."

THE COST AND THE JOY OF DISCIPLESHIP

Luke 5:27-39

LEARNING MENU

Keeping in mind the ways in which your class members learn best as well as their needs and interests, choose at least one learning segment from each of the three Dimensions.

Dimension 1:
What Does the Bible Say?

(A) Read the text.

- Before actually reading the text, ask someone in the class to summarize it.
- Invite other class members to add details that were missed until you have generally reconstructed the story.
- Invite a class member to read aloud the text.

(B) Recall common themes.

During the past week, in their Daily Bible Journey Plan, the class will have read Luke 4:16–6:26.

- Ask class members to list any common themes or phrases they see appearing in the text for today that were also in others that they have read as part of their Journey. (Note the phrase "left everything," appears here and also in 5:11. The theme of controversy over whether and how the law is to be obeyed appears repeatedly in the healing miracles. It appears here in the question of eating with sinners. It appears in the next chapter in the questions regarding the sabbath.)
- Record answers on newsprint. Use them later as a reminder of the gist of this entire section in Luke.

Dimension 2:
What Does the Bible Mean?

(C) Understand attitudes regarding tax collectors.

- Summarize some of the information found in the Additional Bible Helps section of this book, page 21.
- Clarify the following information:
- —Tax collectors were despised, first of all, because most of them exploited the people; secondly, because they were seen as traitors and foreign agents; and, thirdly, because in their close association with Gentiles they did not always keep the law as strictly as the Pharisees would have wished.

—Clearly, the occupation was very different from that of a modern agent of the Internal Revenue Service. Today, although we may dislike the impersonal nature of the IRS, and we may joke about it, we all know that taxes are passed by a Congress whom we elect, and that the agents charged with the task of collecting them are employees of the government. They have been screened by the Civil Service and are subject to regulations to keep them from abusing their power or exploiting us.

—If IRS agents use their authority as a means to enrich themselves, there are avenues for protest and redress. In ancient times, tax collectors (also called "publicans") collected taxes on which the people had no say, imposed by the Roman government on all people except Romans. (Remember what was said about taxes in chapter 2.) To make matters worse, tax collectors had no salary, but lived off what they could skim from the taxes they collected. Little wonder they were so despised!

● Ask the question:

—What occupation or occupations today would be similar to that of a first century tax collector? (In some ways, perhaps the best answer is that tax collectors were like drug dealers, who make money by creating greater misery in the community. Although many tax collectors came from the communities where they collected taxes, and although they often were rich, they certainly were not admired as pillars of the community. Is this not the case of drug dealers today?)

(D) Pretend to be Levi.

● Ask the members of the class to pretend that they are Levi.

● Instruct members to write a letter of invitation to a colleague asking him or her to come to a banquet in honor of Jesus and announcing that he or she is "quitting the business."

● When sufficient time has been allowed for class members to write their invitation, ask these questions:

—What would Levi say about Jesus, hoping that his colleague would understand?

—What would he say about himself and his decision?

Option as an additional point to activity (D):

● Invite two members of the class to portray two tax collectors who have received the invitation and ask them to improvise a dialogue about it.

● Invite two members of the class to portray two Pharisees who have heard about this banquet. Instruct them to improvise a dialogue about "that Levi and his kind." (They may choose to walk over to Levi's house, see what is going on, and comment on it.)

● Explain that banquets in the first century were quite elaborate and expensive. For Levi to invite a large crowd must have been quite an expense. The word in Greek that Luke uses, and the word that the NRSV translates as "sitting at the table," actually means "reclining." This was a formal banquet with all the most elegant practices of the time.

(E) Consider the relationships of publicans and Pharisees.

● Before class invite a member to research information on "Pharisee" and "publican" (or "tax collector"). Use Bible dictionaries that may be located in your church or public library or your pastor's study.

● Invite the class member who has researched information in advance to share why a Pharisee would object to Jesus eating at the home of a tax collector.

● If it is possible, invite the class member to report researched information as if he or she were actually a Pharisee.

● Read the words of Jesus in verse 31.

● Ask the class member reporting to respond to Jesus' words recorded in verse 31.

● Highlight the dilemma:

—The Pharisees were either well or sick. If well, Jesus was not for them, and they should have left him alone as he tended to the sick. If sick, they had no reason to consider themselves better than Levi and his guests.

—Throughout the Gospel of Luke and the Book of Acts, the topics of wealth and its use are important. Fred Craddock says in his book, *Luke* (from the Interpretation series of commentaries; John Knox, 1990; page 77):

"Unlike many preachers who wait for the rich and powerful to experience a reversal of fortune before speaking to them of God's reign, Jesus' word to the rich and powerful *creates* the reversal of their lives: 'He left everything and followed him.' "

—What Craddock says is very different from the "gospel of success" (heard so often on radio and television) that if we follow Jesus we shall prosper materially.

● Ask the questions:

—Is Craddock right?

—Why is it that we do not often hear this idea expressed in the preaching of the Gospel?

(F) Look at the joy of following Jesus.

● Before class, assign a member of the class to skim through the Gospel of Luke and count how many times Jesus is depicted as eating or attending a banquet. (You may suggest the use of a concordance, where one could look up words such as "eat," "feast," or "banquet." In Luke, more than in any other Gospel, Jesus is often eating or attending banquets and meals.)

- Hear the report of the class member.
- Discuss what Jesus may have meant by his reference to the "bridegroom" (34) and to his being now with them and later taken away (35). (Clearly, Jesus was saying that this was a time for celebration, even though later things would be different.)

(G) Explore new wineskins.

You may wish to refer to the section on Additional Bible Helps, pages 21-22, regarding the difference between Luke's usage of the "new patch" image, and the way Matthew and Mark used it.

- Discuss why it would not be a good idea to put "new wine" in old wineskins.
—Suppose you had a new garment and an old one that was torn. Would you tear the new in order to mend the old?
—What did Jesus mean by this?
—Was he saying merely that the new is better than the old?
—Was he saying also that there are times when, in order to choose the new, you have to give up the old entirely?

(H)) Discover another image.

- Prior to class, buy several sets of metric nuts and bolts, all the same size, and an equal number of non-metric nuts, almost exactly the same size. (If you are using these materials only for this option, two or three sets will suffice. But if you are using it also in Dimension 3, you will need one set for each person in the class.)
- Distribute the metric bolts and the non-metric nuts.
- Instruct class members to put the nuts and bolts together.(The two will look as if they should fit, but they will not. It may even be possible to turn the nut a bit, but it will not go on. If so, your point will be even clearer.)
- Hand out the metric nuts. They will fit on the metric bolts.
- Share:
—The point should be clear: If you would use the new metric system, you cannot simply fit it into the old. Although it is clear that the metric system makes calculations much simpler than the traditional system, many are having a hard time converting into metric. Why? Perhaps because we have a vast investment in non-metric machinery and equipment, and much of this would be lost.

- Discuss:
—Could this be what Jesus meant when he told the Pharisees that, having drunk of the old wine, they did not desire the new?
- Collect the nuts and bolts.

Dimension 3:
What Does the Bible Mean to Us?

(I) Discover how we are like Bible characters.

- On three different pieces of newsprint, write, as a heading, the words: "Levi," "the Pharisees and their scribes," and "the disciples."
- Ask the class to list some of the ways in which we are or may be like each of these three. (Make certain that the class considers all three of them. For instance, if they insist that we tend to be like the Pharisees, ask them if there are any ways in which we are like Levi, or like the disciples. Or, if they say simply that we are like the disciples because we believe in Jesus, insist on their finding points of contact with Levi and with the Pharisees.)
- After this discussion, ask the following questions:
—Why do you think the title for this lesson is "The Cost and the Joy of Discipleship"?
—Can you list some of the costs?
—Can you list some of the joys?
—How can we make certain that we pay the cost without losing the joy?

(J) Read the newspapers.

- Gather and bring to class several newspapers.
- In small groups, scan both religious sections and general news for mention of the word *Christian*. Note also any petitions for Christians to defend morality or to oppose immoral causes.
- Discuss the question:
—On the basis of the passage we are studying, what do you think Jesus would have to say about this particular use of the word *Christian* as raised in particular news articles?

(K) Consider who our tax collectors are.

The study book states that quite often the reason why churches hesitate to begin new ministries is fear. They are ready to welcome "outsiders" and even "sinners," as long as there are not so many of "them" as to overwhelm us.

We can well imagine that the Pharisees would have no objection to Levi's changing his ways. But when he began inviting his old cronies, that was just too much!

- Discuss these questions:
—Who are the equivalent of the tax collectors in our community?
—Are we really proclaiming the gospel to them?
—Are we showing them the same acceptance Jesus showed Levi and his friends?
—Is there anything we should do differently?
—Where can we start?

(L) Identify obstacles to discipleship.

- Distribute a non-metric nut to each class member.
- Tell members that non-metric nuts are part of old paradigms, just as were old wineskins and old patches in Jesus' day.
- Invite members to think for several moments about what in their personal lives represents the "old" and blocks their faithful discipleship.
- Ask each member to "name" the nut they are holding, giving it the name of that which they feel they must leave behind, although they may not be ready to do so. (Class members should do this silently.)
- Suggest that class members put the nut with their coins or pocket change and that they continue carrying it until they are ready to give up the "old" that it represents. Whenever they reach for a coin, this nut is to remind them of their call to discipleship, like Jesus calling Levi.
- When members are finally ready to set aside whatever the nut represents (following Levi's example, who left everything and followed Jesus), they may also get rid of the nut.
- End the class with an open invitation:

If at any time any of you decide that the time has come when you can be rid of whatever stands in the way of your discipleship, and you wish to celebrate that moment, feel free to have a celebration! You do not have to tell us what it was that you found a hindrance in your discipleship. Just call us, and, as disciples of the same Lord of the Banquet, we will come and celebrate with you!

Additional Bible Helps

Tax Collectors

The following two quotations will help you understand and explain how people reacted to tax collectors.

- "The task of collecting taxes was usually given to a wealthy and powerful figure in a geographical area, most often someone who was not a native of that area. He in turn divided the area into tax districts with chief collectors who in turn used locals for the actual collec-

tions. The system allowed for extra tax to be collected above the amount to be sent to the government. The doors to corruption stood wide open. In the literature of the period, including the New Testament, publicans were despised. Add to the financial oppression the ceremonial impurity of such contact with Gentiles and the element of treason for working with foreigners against one's own people and the outcast status is understandable" (*Luke*, by Fred B. Craddock; page 77).

- "During the republic and the early years of the empire, most of these taxes were collected by tax farmers known as 'publicans.' Since substantial capital was required, most publican entrepreneurs were rich members of the equestrian class, who often joined in veritable holding companies. They contracted with the government to raise the taxes of a particular area and to collect a fee for this service. This fee, however, was only part of their profit. Since many agricultural taxes were collected in kind, publicans made large profits by reselling the goods collected or by hoarding them until prices rose. They also served the central government as its financial agents in the provinces, employing the goods and funds that they held in order to cover such expenses as salaries and supplies for the legions. Since all this was done by means of paper transactions, it saved much of the costly and dangerous transport of goods and money.

"Little government bureaucracy was in place, and therefore publicans also served as government agents in managing public works and providing some postal service. Naturally, for this also they charged a fee. When a farmer could not pay his taxes, publicans would often lend him money at annual rates that varied from 12 to 48 percent. Such loans grew rapidly as interest and new tax liabilities accumulated, and eventually the land was confiscated by the publicans. Beyond these various legal means of profit, some publicans would also take advantage of the ignorance and powerlessness of taxpayers, assessing them more than they should or undervaluing their contributions. Thus the negative image of publicans found in the Gospels was probably shared by much of the populace of the Roman provinces" (*Faith and Wealth*, by Justo L. González; Harper & Row, 1990; page 38).

Gospel Differences Regarding the Old and the New

There is a difference in the passage regarding the old and new cloth between Luke on the one hand, and Matthew and Mark on the other. Since the version of Matthew and Mark is the most commonly known, you should be aware of the two versions.

In Matthew 9:16 and Mark 2:21, the contrast is not between an old and a new garment, as in Luke (5:36), but rather between an old cloth and a piece of unshrunk cloth.

What Matthew and Mark say is that, if one tries to mend

a tear in an old piece of cloth with a new one that has not yet shrunk, when the new piece shrinks it will tear the old. Thus, the image is exactly parallel to that of the new wine bursting the old wineskins.

In Luke, the two images are different. The reference to the wine and the wineskins does make the point that the power of the new will break the old. The reference to the two garments makes a slightly different point. If you try to put together the old and the new indiscriminately, you will lose both the old and the new.

Finally, the very last verse in Luke (39) appears in neither Matthew nor Mark. You may be helped in the interpretation of this verse by the following:

"The final parabolic statement—found only in Luke—reminds us again of the capacity of this message to repel as well as to attract, and the way in which the visitation of the prophet creates a division within the people. Those who are most accustomed to the old wine will not even taste the new; the old, they say, is good enough. To drink the new wine offered at Jesus' banquet, to wear the new garment for his wedding feast, one must have a new heart, go through *metanoia*, a change of mind, such as that shown by tax-agents and sinners" (*The Gospel of Luke*, by Luke Timothy Johnson, The Liturgical Press, 1991; page 100).

5

A LIFE-GIVING SABBATH

Luke 6:1-11

LEARNING MENU

Keep in mind the ways in which your class members learn best as you choose one or more teaching methods from Dimensions 1, 2, and 3.

Dimension 1:
What Does the Bible Say?

(A) Read the text.

Read aloud Luke 6:1-11.

(B) Interpret the law.

● Share the following information:

—Most readers, upon first coming upon the passage about Jesus' disciples picking grain from the field, will react by thinking that they were stealing. That is not what is at stake here, and if there is the possibility that your study group might understand the story in terms of property rights and theft, you may wish to spend some time clarifying the matter.

—The law clearly stipulated that the hungry could go into a neighbor's field or vineyard, and take whatever one needed to eat. This was based on Israel's understanding of the ownership of land and the rights of the poor.

● If your study group meets for more than an hour at a time, you may have the time to discuss this issue further. Additional Bible Helps, page 27, provides further information. If your group meets for less than an hour, you may simply wish to state that this practice was allowed under Hebrew law, and then move on to the main theme of the session.

(C) Consider what is legal today.

● Share the following incident:

—You are driving along a citrus grove in Florida and see the car ahead of you stop. The people get out, jump over a fence, and start eating fruit.

● Ask the question:

—Is this legal? (Explain that, under the law of Israel in the time of Jesus, it would have been. Gathering food from the field was quite acceptable in a land where there were few or no places to buy food along the road. In the law of the Old Testament, there was always provision made so that the poor would not starve. Therefore, anyone who was hungry had the right to go into a field and eat—but this law did not include carrying food away.)

(D) Look at the setting.

- Draw the attention of the group to the setting of the two stories we are studying. Ask:
—Does the text actually say in what order these two events took place? (Obviously, one appears after the other, and therefore the immediate assumption is that they occurred in that order. But the text does not say so. All it says is "one sabbath," and "in another sabbath.")

Dimension 2:
What Does the Bible Mean?

The study book makes two, equally important, points:
(1) The text does not say that the sabbath is bad, nor that it should be abandoned;
(2) The text does say that there are other considerations besides the mere keeping of the rules regarding the sabbath.

It is important to make both points, for otherwise we can readily assume that the problem with the sabbath was that it was a bad rule, and that all we have to do is get rid of this bad rule and any others. If, however, the sabbath was a good rule—indeed, if it was commanded by God, as the Bible clearly says—then the question is much more difficult.

(E) Discuss the importance of the sabbath.

- Ask a class member to read the sidebar from Exodus 20 in the study book, page 37. This is one of the Ten Commandments.
- Ask the class:
—Do you think that Jesus was against the keeping of the sabbath?
—Does the text we are studying say so? Is there any passage in the New Testament that says so? (Obviously, the answer is no. Jesus was, not only a Jew, but a good Jew. He obeyed the law of Israel. He kept the sabbath. In this passage, however, he clashed with the Pharisees on the question of the sabbath—not on whether it ought to be kept, but on *how* it ought to be kept.)
—What were the points of disagreement between Jesus and the Pharisees when it came to the keeping of the sabbath? (Apparently, the main point of disagreement was that Jesus was not willing to make the sabbath, and in particular all the minute rules regarding it, the final criterion for his action. The sabbath was there for serving God and God's creation. If it became an obstacle, it was not serving its proper function.)

(F) Learn about the Pharisees.

Since the Pharisees play such an important role in this story, and in several others in the Gospel of Luke, you may wish to spend some time clarifying who they were.

- Research the topic "Pharisee" in a Bible dictionary such as *The Interpreter's Dictionary of the Bible*, volume 3, available in many church libraries or perhaps your pastor's study. Briefly share information from your research at this point in the lesson.
—The Pharisees were not bad people. On the contrary, they were good, religious people. The problem was that, in their very goodness, they left little room for grace and for God's goodness to those who were not as obedient nor as meticulous as they were.
- Discuss the following questions:
—We are religious people who are interested in studying Scripture and in making it the guide for our lives. Do we run the risk of being like the Pharisees?
—What can we do to avoid it?

(G) Compare two Bible stories.

The text we are studying consists of two stories: Luke 6:1-5 and 6:6-11.

- Divide the class in two groups. Ask each group to study one of the two stories.
- Then ask the following questions in order to compare and contrast the stories.
—When did this happen? (Both on the sabbath day.)
—Where did this happen? (One in the fields, the other in the synagogue. In other words, the religious element was stronger and more directly present in the second than in the first story.)
—For whose benefit did Jesus "break" the law? (In the first story, he and his disciples were eating. It was for their own benefit. In the second story, it was for the benefit of the man with the withered hand.)
—Who were the adversaries in each story? (In the first, the Pharisees; in the second, the scribes and Pharisees. This further shows that the stakes were higher in the second story.)
—By whose action did Jesus justify his actions? (In the first story, by David's action. In the second, by his own action in healing the man.)
- Ask each group to study the last verse of their story. (Ask the first group to study also the parallel verses in Mark 2:27-28 and Matthew 12:8.)
—Most scholars are agreed that both Luke and Matthew used Mark as one of their main sources. In a way, both Matthew and Luke are expansions of Mark. Here, however, both Matthew and Luke omit something that Mark says: "The sabbath was made for humankind, and not humankind for the sabbath" (27).
—By omitting that line, Luke clarified that Jesus

claimed authority over the sabbath, not generally as a human being, but also and very specifically as "the Son of Man." That helps to explain the animosity of the Pharisees.

- Ask the second group to comment on what they see as the reaction of the scribes and Pharisees.
—You may wish to tell them that what the Greek literally says, and the NRSV translates as "they were filled with fury" is "they were filled with mindlessness." In other words, they were so angry they were beside themselves.
- Conclude this option with a discussion as to whether the class sees a progress in the conflict between Jesus and the religious leaders of his time.

Dimension 3:
What Does the Bible Mean to Us?

Two points were made in the study book: (1) the first had to do with the sabbath and the need for rest; (2) the second had to do with the danger of using good rules in bad ways.

There is value for us in the ancient law regarding the sabbath. At this point, it is important to distinguish between the sabbath as it is described in the Ten Commandments and much of what people mean today when they speak of "the sabbath." In the Ten Commandments, the sabbath was essentially a day of rest. Eventually, it became the day when people gathered at the synagogue. From that latter connection, Christians have often confused the day of rest (the sabbath proper) with the day of worship. This understanding is true of "sabbatarian" Christians, who insist on keeping Saturday as "the sabbath," and of others who often refer to Sunday as "the sabbath." In fact, although the two understandings are related, they are not necessarily the same. In ancient Israel, the sabbath was marked by special acts of worship; but its essence was rest. In the early church, people continued keeping the sabbath as the day of rest, and Sunday as the day for celebrating the resurrection of the Lord. Although we may combine these two dimensions, it is important not to confuse them.

(H) Research the meaning of *sabbath*.

- If some members of your class are interested in doing this type of research, ask them to look up the term *sabbath* in both a Bible dictionary and a more general dictionary on Christian history (such as *The Oxford Dictionary of the Christian Church* or *The Dictionary of Bible and Religion*). Give class members time to report during class, and allow their reports to be discussed briefly.

(I) Consider our understandings of the sabbath.

- Distribute paper and pencil among the class members.
- Ask each member to write a brief diary of what they did each of the last ten days. (These could be no more than one sentence descriptions of each day's activities, such as "Went to work," "Mowed the lawn in the morning and went shopping in the afternoon.")
- After all have written their reports, ask if anyone wrote, for any one day "Did nothing."
- Discuss responses to the following questions:
—Does this mean that we have forgotten how to rest?
—Do we know how to enjoy leisure without filling it with activity?
—Could it be that, even when we simply lie on a couch and watch a football game, we are avoiding the true rest of simply doing nothing?
- Read the sabbath commandment, as it appears in the sidebar in the study book, page 41.
- Ask the class:
—Suppose that we were to take this commandment seriously, and spend a day every week doing nothing, really doing nothing. How would that change our lives?
—Could we actually do nothing, or are we so programmed for activity that we would find it impossible?
—If we were able to do nothing, what would be the results?
—Suppose that several of us began taking that commandment seriously, and we rested one day every week. What would be the result in society?
—Might we rediscover dimensions in life that we have forgotten?
—Might we become more humane? (Ancient Israel believed that was the case.)

The second point in the study book speaks to the danger of using good rules in bad ways. Use the following activities for learnings in this area.

(J) Remember the parable of the good Samaritan.

- Read the parable of the good Samaritan (Luke 10:25-37).
- Discuss these questions:
—Do you think that the people who did not stop were simply callous?
—Were they people who did not care for the man in need?
—Were they people who were following other rules that prevented them from being contaminated by touching a man that could possibly be dead? (One advantage of this learning segment is that it will give you a chance to look at a parable that appears only in Luke, but that we shall not have the opportunity to study in detail in this series.)

- You may wish to look at a Bible commentary on Luke, in order to see something of the rules that would keep the priest and the Levite from touching a bleeding and possibly dead man.

(K) Tell a story.

- Tell the following story:

    A family was getting ready to leave for church. Their young son (ten years old) was already dressed in his Sunday clothes. He was told to take care not to soil his clothes. The parents went upstairs to get dressed, while the son waited in the living room. The boy looked out the window and saw that his dog was all muddy and bleeding from a cut. He went out, got the dog, washed it, and tried to dress a wound. When the parents came down, ready to rush off to church, here was the boy, all muddy, with the dog resting on his lap.

- Ask the class members to imagine that they are the boy's parents.
—What do you think you would say to your son?
—Would you punish him for being disobedient?
—Would you try to help him with the dog?
—Would you take your son with you to church just as he is?
—Would you give him a chance to change clothes even though that would mean that you will all be late?
—Which of these various responses do you think would better express your Christian faith?

There is no right answer to these questions, and much depends on the motivation for your response. (For instance, you may take the boy to church just as he is because you are proud of what he did, or you may do the same because you wish to punish and humiliate him.) A discussion of this very simple story will help to show how complicated these issues are.

(L) Define the purpose of rules.

- Give each person six wooden matches.
- Ask each class member to arrange the matches in such a way that they form four equilateral triangles, all the same size.
- Allow several moments for members to attempt the arrangement. (Solution: You must build a pyramid with the matches, with three matches to form a triangle at the base, and one match coming up from each of the corners of the triangle. As long as you think in terms of a flat surface, the assignment cannot be done. When you add the vertical dimension, the solution becomes quite easy.
- Explain that the same is true in the life of obedience to God. If we take principles as flat rules, we shall soon find that it is impossible to obey them all, for at various points they will clash with each other. If we remember that they are all under God—that there is this other

dimension to our obedience—then obedience will be made possible. Ask if in some sense that is not what Jesus meant when he said that "the Son of Man is Lord of the sabbath."

(M) Examine Jesus' reasons for disobeying the sabbath law.

- Discuss the following question: What reasons did Jesus give for disobeying the law of the sabbath as the Pharisees understood it? (In the first story, it was his own lordship over the sabbath, which presumably was even greater than David's. In the second story, it was the need to give life and health, even though it was the sabbath.) These are probably the same reasons why today we must respect laws and rules, and at the same time be willing to set them aside if necessary.
- Make the following points:
—Our ultimate obedience is not to the laws, but to the Lord of the laws.
—The Lord of the laws is a God of love and life, who does not wish people to die nor to suffer.
- Remind the class of the example given in their material, regarding traffic lights.
- Ask members if they can think of any experiences they have had when it was necessary for them "to run a red light," so to speak, in order to do what had to be done. (Make it very clear, however, that both rules and traffic lights are good and necessary, and that one better not go around disregarding them at will.)
- Ask the following questions:
—Can you think of a similar situation in the life of the church? (Think, for instance, of a church that decided to change its time of worship in order to make room for a shelter for the homeless. Or think of a church that, when an emergency strikes, decides to make use of its building as a medical center, even though the rules of its denomination require that this be approved by a series of committees (which would probably delay the response and cause undue suffering to those who are hurting.)
—What do you think we would do in such circumstances?
—Would we stand with the scribes and the Pharisees, insisting on the literal observance of all rules?
—Would we stand with the God who wishes for us to save life, not to destroy it?

Additional Bible Helps

On the Pharisees

Unfortunately, in our time the word *Pharisee* has become an insult, holding the general meaning of "hypocrite." That meaning is unfortunate, because the Pharisees were probably the best and most religious people in Israel in the time of Jesus. One of the many results of Israel's difficult history was that worship in the Temple had become more and more difficult for the masses, and that much of the ancient law needed constant reinterpretation. That law had been given under different circumstances, for a people whose political, economic, and social life was very different. Now in the first century under Roman rule and being part of the vast economy of the Mediterranean basin, there were Jews who worried that their ancient laws needed to be made to bear on their daily lives.

Contrary to what we often imagine, the Pharisees were concerned with the meaning of faith for daily life. That was precisely why they spent so much time and effort examining the law, in order to see what was permitted and what was not. They believed that God was still active, and had been active throughout the history of Israel. They believed that God's revealed word was not limited to the ancient five books of the Law, but included also other books written at a later time.

If Jesus had such harsh words to say to them, it was not because they were evil, but because they were good, religious people. Jesus opposed them, not because they were not religious, but because they were often tempted to act as if their religion made them intrinsically better that others.

It is important for us to remember this fact for two reasons. First, modern Judaism is derived mostly from Phariseism, and therefore to misunderstand Phariseism is also to misunderstand modern Judaism. Second, when we understand why Jesus clashed with the Pharisees, we begin to see that it is precisely those of us who are most religious, sincere, and decent folk who are most susceptible to the same flaws for which Jesus faulted the ancient Pharisees.

On Land and the Rights of the Poor
One of the elements of this lesson that may be new to some is the degree to which the ancient law of Israel made room for feeding the poor and the needy. According to the law of Israel, the land did not ultimately belong to those who held it as property, rather it belonged to God. Since God was the ultimate owner, part of the produce of the land had to be reserved for the poor, the orphaned, the widows, and the sojourners—people who otherwise lacked the protection of others. This law included the right that the disciples of Jesus were exercising in this passage—to take from a field whatever one needed when one was hungry. There actually was a debate among the rabbis as to how this law applied when the traveler was not poor. The

traveler had obviously taken what belonged to the poor. Should restitution be made? Some believed the answer to be yes. Others argued that, since at the time of taking the food the traveler was needy, no restitution had to be made.

This law was not a matter of charity. The poor and the needy had rights. For instance, the edges of a field of grain could not be harvested by the owner, for they belonged to the poor. Likewise, the harvesters could not go a second time over a particular field, for anything that was overlooked or dropped in the first pass belonged to the poor. This commandment was so important, and so debated, that the Talmud devotes an entire tract to it. How much must be left, was clearly regulated by law. Thus, what Jesus and his disciples took and ate from the field literally belonged to them. It was their right to take this as sojourners that they were. (See *Faith and Wealth*, by Justo González; pages 20-23.)

On the Sabbath and Sunday Worship
The reason why the early church began gathering together on Sundays had nothing to do with the sabbath. They gathered on Sundays, because that was the day of the resurrection of the Lord, and Christian worship was essentially a celebration of the Resurrection.

As long as the majority of Christians were also Jews, they continued keeping the sabbath. Soon the majority of Christians were Gentiles, and at that point, the custom of keeping the day of rest fell into disuse. This pattern became even stronger, since many Christians were people, such as slaves, who could not determine when they would work and when they would not. Therefore, from the very beginning Sunday was the day in which Christians gathered for worship. Since this was not necessarily a day of rest, their services usually took place early in the morning, before the beginning of the workday.

After the Empire became Christian, with the conversion of Emperor Constantine (fourth century), laws were passed making Sunday a day of celebration and of rest. It was much later, especially after the Reformation, that some Christians began referring to Sunday as "the sabbath." Eventually this gave rise to a movement that insisted that the sabbath should be on Saturday. This is the origin of the various "sabbatarian" movements. They are historically right in that the sabbath was celebrated on Saturday. They are also mistaken, in confusing the Christian day of worship, which is a celebration of the Lord's resurrection, with the ancient sabbath, which was above all a day of rest.

6

THE PHARISEE AND THE FORGIVEN WOMAN

Luke 7:36-50

LEARNING MENU

Keeping in mind the ways in which your class members learn best as well as their needs and interests, choose at least one learning segment from each of the three Dimensions.

As the student material points out, the story we are studying is often confused with a similar story that appears also (in three slightly different versions) in Matthew, Mark, and John. In spite of those similarities, however, this seems to be an altogether different story, and it certainly makes a different point.

Dimension 1:
What Does the Bible Say?

(A) Recall the story.

- Invite students to tell the story of the woman who anointed Jesus' feet, when he ate at the home of Simon the Pharisee. Encourage class members to recall as many details as they can.
- As each detail is given, write it on newsprint or on the chalkboard. Chances are you will get details such as the

woman's name (Mary, or Mary Magdalene), the fact that the ointment was expensive, that Judas protested, that Jesus said, "the poor you have always with you," and so forth.
- Invite a class member to read the story aloud. As the reading takes place, make a check mark by each detail that is mentioned in your list. Start a separate list with any details in the Lukan story that you did not have on your previous list.
- At the end of the reading, ask the following question:
—Why do you think we thought we knew all these details, and actually took for granted that we would find them in this story?
- Divide the class into three groups. To each group assign one Bible passage, each of which present another story: Matthew 26:6-13; Mark 14:3-9; John 12:1-8).
- Discuss:
—Do reading these passages tell us where we might have gotten other bits of "information"? Remind class members that your study will be based on Luke's story and not on the other one that appears in the other Gospels.

(B) Compare Bible versions.

- Select four people. Invite them to read aloud each of the four texts that deal with a woman anointing Jesus (Luke 7:36-50; Matthew 26:6-13; Mark 14:3-9; and John 12:1-8).

28

- Compare the two versions found in Matthew and Mark. (They are clearly the same story, with some minor variations.)
- Ask the person who has been assigned the passage from John to read it aloud.
- Again, compare this passage with the other two. (The class will find that, although there are significant differences, this is still the same story.)
- Finally, read the passage from Luke aloud. Read it slowly, no more than one verse at a time. After each verse, ask the following questions:
—Is this different from the other story we have been discussing?
—How is it different?
—Is this particular detail (for instance, that Simon was a Pharisee) in that other story?
- At the end of the reading, ask these questions:
—What elements or details are missing from this story that were present in the other one? (For instance, there is no mention here of giving the money to the poor, or of the disciples being present, or of the anointing being a sign of Jesus' death.)
—What important elements in this story are completely missing in the other? (Jesus' host thought that Jesus was no prophet; Jesus allowed this woman to touch him; Jesus told a parable to his host; Jesus' host had been ungracious.)
- At the end of this process, indicate that the story in Luke is really a different story from the one in the other Gospels, and that it is making a different point. The rest of the session will try to concentrate on this particular story, without allowing the other one to confuse or obscure it.

Dimension 2: What Does the Bible Mean?

Your purpose here is to help the group understand the development and the thrust of the story—to get into it in such a way that they can then apply it to their lives.

(C) Consider Simon the Pharisee.

One way of approaching this text is to concentrate on Simon the Pharisee—both on what the story leads us to expect of him, and on what he might have been thinking and saying.
- Read verse 36 aloud. Ask:
—When Luke tells us that Jesus' host was a Pharisee, what images come to mind?
- Record on newsprint or chalkboard any recollections of class members regarding the Pharisees, which may have been gathered from previous lessons. (Luke allows us to

get the impression that this Pharisee was different somehow. After all, didn't he invite Jesus to eat at his house?)
- Retell briefly what Luke says in verses 37-38, and read verse 39 aloud.
- Ask the class:
—What else have we learned about the Pharisee and his attitude? (There is a clear distinction between what the text actually says, and what we may surmise. For instance, the text says that he came to the conclusion that Jesus was not a prophet, since he could not tell that the woman was a sinner. We may surmise that he was disappointed, for he really expected Jesus to be a prophet. We may also surmise that he had never really believed in Jesus and his authority, and that now he was glad to see his opinion confirmed. So far, the text has not given us a hint in one direction or the other. You may also wish to explain that the Pharisee's concern about "who is touching him" had much to do with his own understanding of ritual purity. If the woman was unclean, as the Pharisee seemed to take for granted, that would make Jesus also unclean. Having allowed her to touch him, he would now have to undergo a process of purification. For that reason, observant Jews were very careful about whom they allowed to touch them. The Pharisee himself would never have allowed this woman, a "sinner," to touch him.)
- Read verses 40-43 aloud. Ask:
—If you were the Pharisee, what would you think about that conversation? (To this point Jesus had given no inkling that he knew the Pharisee's inner thoughts. As far as the Pharisee was concerned, either Jesus was making idle chat, or he was talking about something that had nothing to do with the present situation. Often a parable's function was to catch the hearer unawares. Think for instance of the parable that Nathan told King David in 2 Samuel 12:1-7. David heard the parable, and was incensed by the rich man's crime. It was then that Nathan told him: "You are the man!" Likewise, here the Pharisee heard the parable without apparently suspecting that it referred to him and to the woman whom he had classified as a "sinner.")
- Read verses 44-46. These are the verses that show the contrast between the woman's actions and the Pharisee's actions.
- Discuss the following questions:
—What have we now learned about the Pharisee and about his attitude toward Jesus?
—How do you think the Pharisee would have felt, having his actions compared with those of the woman whom he scorned?
—How would he feel, in a society where hospitality was so important, being told that his hospitality lacked even the basic courtesies?
- Read verse 47. This was the last time that Jesus addressed his host. Up to this point, Simon had no

inkling what this was all about. Now the parable came home to roost. It was like Nathan saying to David: "You are the man!" In a few words, Jesus made the meaning of the parable clear, showed the Pharisee why the woman was closer to God than he was, and told his host that he knew all along what he was thinking. Make certain that the class sees the irony: The Pharisee was telling himself that Jesus must not be a prophet, for he did not know about the woman's sin. All along, Jesus knew, not only about the woman, but also what the Pharisee was thinking! After this point Luke simply ignored the Pharisee, who was not mentioned again.

(D) Consider the woman.

● Consider the perspective of the woman. Ask,
—What did it take for this woman to come into this banquet and do what she did? (The section in Additional Bible Helps states that it was fairly impossible for her to come into the banquet at all. Clearly, it must have taken an overwhelming sense of gratitude and love for her to "crash" the party. We do not know who the woman was, and therefore we have no idea why she felt such gratitude toward Jesus. This is one of the reasons why some people have thought that the woman was Mary Magdalene, "from whom seven demons had gone out." See Luke 8:3.)

(E) Roleplay the action.

● Invite three or four members of the class to act as if they were among the Pharisee's other guests, telling a friend what had happened at the banquet.
● After the roleplay, compare their account with what Luke tells us.

Dimension 3:
What Does the Bible Mean to Us?

This is a difficult text to apply to our lives, for few of us consider ourselves as sinful as apparently did the woman, nor as smug and safe as did the Pharisee. Yet, there are a number of ways in which you can invite discussion and reflection on this text and its meaning for us.

(F) Explore what it means to have Jesus as a guest.

Help the class to think about what it would mean to have Jesus as a guest. In the Dominican Republic there was a very cruel and feared dictator by the name of Rafael Leonidas Trujillo. After Trujillo died, his palace was opened to the public. There, hanging above the desk from

which he must have ordered many a summary execution, was a sign: "Jesus is the unseen guest at our table; unheard listener to our conversation; unseen witness to our deeds." It is hard to believe that the dictator really believed what the sign said, or his life and his government would have been very different.
● Discuss the following questions:
—Do we really believe that Jesus is our unseen guest at table and throughout life?
—What difference does it make, if any, to have Jesus at our table?
—Are we like Simon the Pharisee, taking secret solace in thinking that Jesus did not really know what was going on?
—What do you think Simon would have done differently if he had not doubted Jesus' ability to discern the situation?
—What would we do differently if Jesus were actually sitting at our table? Why don't we?

(G) Explore a modern example.

● Share the following scenario:
Suppose that you are in the middle of a Sunday morning worship service. As the choir finishes singing, someone walks in. We all know that he is the town bum. He has never been to church before. As a matter of fact, he would often mock and curse those who went to church. He walks down the aisle and kneels at the altar. He is crying. He obviously is in an emotional state.
● Ask the group to suppose they were leading the worship service. They were about to introduce the preacher. They have several options:
a) Ignore the man and continue as if he were not there.
b) Ask the ushers to escort him out of the church.
c) Kneel next to him and pray with him while the preacher and the rest of the congregation fend for themselves.
d) Ask another member of the congregation to take the man into another room and pray with him.
e) Give the man an opportunity to speak.
f) Employ some other option.
● Ask these questions:
—Which of these options would you follow? Why?
—How would our congregation react to each of those options?
—Does the story of Jesus and the woman at the home of Simon have anything to tell us about this situation?

(H) Hold a debate.

One of the elements in this story is the woman's eagerness to express her love and gratitude. She did so even though it might have cost her some embarrassment, and even though she probably knew that she would not be welcomed by Simon the Pharisee. We sorely need this example today. We hear constant complaints that church membership is dwindling. Seldom do we acknowledge the fact that if that is the case, it is partly because we ourselves fail to give effective witness. We are embarrassed to speak about our faith, to tell someone what Jesus means to us, and what Jesus has done for us.

In the story we are studying, the woman's gratitude and love were expressed in her tears and her actions. Obviously, there are other ways to express our love and gratitude to our Savior.

- Set up a debate. Appoint two teams of two persons each.
- Each person may have three minutes to argue their position.
- Ask one team to defend the proposition: It is possible to be a faithful Christian without ever talking about it to others.
- Discuss as a class the positions raised in the debate.

(I) Write a contemporary short story.

- Distribute paper and pencil, and ask the class to write a very short story that somehow makes the same points as the story in Luke. It should be a modern story, set in a contemporary situation. The situation could be in our church, in our home, or in our workplace. The important point is to preserve what each person thinks is the main point of Luke's story.
- For example, using the story appearing in learning segment (G), it would be possible to write a short story about when the town bum came to church, crying and quite emotional, and how people in church reacted.
- After each person has written his or her own short story, divide the class into groups of three. In these triads, encourage members to share what each has written.

Optional Method: Since what you wish to attain is not a literary piece, but rather the process of thinking about what the story in Luke might mean if set in today's circumstances, you may find that the discussion moves more swiftly if you eliminate writing the story and simply verbalize the activity.

Additional Bible Helps

Importance of Meals

The importance of meals in the Gospel of Luke was explored in lesson 4, page 19 of this leader's guide. Refer again to this information as you prepare this lesson. This is not the last time that we shall find Jesus at table in our journey with Luke.

An Uninvited Guest

One question that your class may find puzzling is how this woman was able to make her way to the dinner table. From our modern perspective, she would appear to be "crashing" the party. But that is not the way things were in ancient times. It was quite common for banquets to be celebrated in courtyards, or even in rooms where the doors were left open in order to allow the air to circulate. In such banquets, people who had not been invited were allowed to beg, or to pick up scraps left by the guests. (You may have been in an open-air cafe in some countries where children come to beg, and where dogs are walking around waiting for something to drop from a table. Apparently, the atmosphere at these ancient banquets was often like that situation—except that, rather than sit at table, people reclined at it.)

In that kind of setting, it would have been quite normal for someone to come in uninvited, together with other beggars. Quite possibly, the woman was not the only uninvited guest present at the banquet.

Laws Regarding Purity

The reason why the Pharisee felt so smug about Jesus allowing the woman to touch him was that there were all sorts of laws about purity and laws about the consequences of what happened if one was touched by an impure (or "unclean") person. (Look up "Clean and Unclean" in a dictionary such as *The Interpreter's Dictionary of the Bible*, Volume One; Abingdon Press, 1984). Uncleanness had both a ritual and a moral dimension. By the time of Jesus the two were combined.

Most importantly, uncleanness was transmitted by contact with an unclean object or person. For that reason, it was customary for Jews who strictly observed their religion to avoid contact with any unclean person or object. Simon the Pharisee presumably would not have allowed the woman to touch him. For one thing, her sinfulness made her unclean. For another, according to the law, both semen and menstrual flow, as well as other bodily discharges, were unclean. Therefore, a good Pharisee such as Simon, not knowing for certain that the woman was ritually clean, and "knowing" that she was morally unclean, would avoid touching her. Jesus apparently allowed her to touch him, kiss his feet, and anoint them with perfume. Therefore, from Simon's perspective, either Jesus did not care much about his own purity, or he had no idea who this woman was!

A Considerable Debt

The figures that Jesus mentioned in his parable, fifty and five hundred denarii, represented a significant amount of money. A denarius was, at least in theory, a worker's daily wage. Thus, both sums were considerable, although one was obviously much larger than the other. For the sake of comparison, it would be something similar to $2,500 and $25,000. The first, though a considerable sum, could conceivably have been forgiven without causing a great stir. The second was a much larger amount, and therefore would have been much harder to forgive. It would have been the equivalent of almost two years' wages.

Apparently the reason why Jesus used these figures was to make it clear that even Simon, who considered himself a good Jew and not much of a sinner, had a considerable debt—even though perhaps the woman's debt was larger.

Who Is This Who Forgives Sins?

"But those who were at the table with him began to say among themselves, 'Who is this who even forgives sins?' " (49) The theme of the forgiveness of sins is central to the Gospel of Luke. According to Luke, that is a crucial aspect of Jesus' mission and teaching. It is the precise issue that caused friction between Jesus and the religious establishment.

Along these lines, you may wish to read Luke 5:17-26. There in that passage the same question was posed, although in a more clearly antagonistic setting: "Who is this who is speaking blasphemies? Who can forgive sins but God alone?" (21) In response to that antagonism, and as proof of his authority, Jesus healed the man.

Here in Luke 7 the question was not clearly antagonistic. It simply may have expressed the puzzlement of those who were present. In any case, Luke did not pick up on it as a subject for controversy, as he did in the previous story. For that reason, Luke did not follow that line of discussion, nor did he have Jesus respond to this particular question.

7

Luke
8:26–56

JESUS HEALS

LEARNING MENU

Keeping in mind the ways in which your class members learn best as well as their needs and interests, choose at least one learning segment from each of the three Dimensions.

Dimension 1:
What Does the Bible Say?

● Your first purpose is to familiarize participants with the biblical text.

(A) Answer the questions in the study book.

● Some classes may wish to
—share and check their answers to the questions on page 52 in the study book during class;
—discuss their answers as part of the class session;
—work on answering the questions during class.
Spend the least amount of time necessary in looking at the questions and answers in Dimension 1.

(B) Tell a story of a miracle.

● Assign three people the task of retelling the story of one of the miracles performed by Jesus. Each should tell the story as if it had happened to her or him. One member should tell the story of the Gerasene demoniac (8:26-39). Another should tell the story of the woman who had suffered from hemorrhages (8:43-48). The third will take on the role of Jairus (8:40-42, 49-56).

● Ask the class members telling the story to tell it as Luke tells it, without embellishments, but as completely as possible. They are not to add anything that is not in the text, and they must try to remember as much detail as they can.

● After each one has told his or her story, read aloud the actual passage in Luke that tells that story. Ask the class to add any corrections that may be necessary in order to get the story as close as possible to what Luke wrote. Remember that all of these stories are closely parallel to Matthew 8:28–9:1 and Mark 5:1-20 (the story of the Gerasene demoniac) and Matthew 9:18-26 and Mark 5:21-43 (the story of Jairus' daughter and the woman with the flow of blood). Be aware that some of the variations in the stories that your "witnesses" tell may have to do with their having read these other versions. If your class time is only one hour, you probably will not have time to compare the various versions. If you have more time, the class may wish to do this same exercise, but with nine different persons, each reading one of the stories from one of the Gospels.

> Optional Method: Use the same method described in activity (B) except have designated class members roleplay the witnesses to the three miracles. For instance, for the story of the Gerasene demoniac, have someone play a swineherd and someone play the role of a person from the city who came to see what the swineherd was talking about. For the story of the woman, have someone play Peter. For the story of Jairus, the witness could be the person who came from Jairus' house to the place where Jesus and Jairus were, and told Jairus that his daughter was dead. (This approach will probably make room for more imaginative reading. Make certain that at this point the class stays fairly close to the biblical text—or at least to some combination of the three Gospel accounts of each of these incidents).

Dimension 2:
What Does the Bible Mean?

(C) Discuss the purpose of the miracles.

- Share the following information:
  Since one of the points that the study book makes is that salvation includes not only spiritual matters but also health and community, you may wish to begin this section with a discussion as to why these passages are in the Bible at all. None of these stories says a word about going to heaven, nor even about forgiveness of sin (as did last week's passage). The stories are about health—mental health, physical health, and even about raising someone from the dead. At no point did Jesus or Luke say anything about "salvation" as we normally understand it.
- Ask these questions:
—Why, then, are these stories in the Bible at all?
  (After some discussion, it is likely that someone will respond that they are in the Bible because they are stories about what Jesus did. That is a good answer. But you can still ask the next question.)
—If Jesus came to save us, why do you think he took the time to heal these people?
  (Someone may respond that he did this so that people would believe his message, as a sort of guarantee or proof that he was indeed who he said he was. However, only in one of these stories did Jesus try to make any use of the miracle as a means to let people know about

him. In the story of the woman, he simply told her that she was healed, and then he let her go. In the case of the daughter of Jairus, he even forbade her family from telling anyone what had taken place.
  Obviously, one answer is that Jesus did these things because he was concerned about people's total well-being. He did not come to save only the soul, but also the body. He healed, because that was part of his mission.)

(D) Translate Greek words.

In the language of the New Testament (Greek), there is only one word which we translate as either "salvation" or "health," according to the context. It derives from a single verb that we translate as either "to save" or "to heal," again according to the context. (The Greek word for "salvation" is *soteria*, and the word for "to save" is *sozo*.) This means that the choice is always up to the translator, and that the difference in the New Testament is not as clear as we sometimes like to make it.

(E) Hear another point of view.

The laws regarding what was clean and what was unclean help us understand the full impact of these stories. In order to bring this point across, follow this procedure:
- A week before class, name someone to be "Devil's advocate" (or, more exactly, "Advocate for the law"). Help this person find materials regarding the laws that determined what and who was clean or unclean. A good starting point will be in looking at the sidebars that appear in the study book. Also, study the topics of "Clean and Unclean" in a good dictionary of the Bible. If in your church library there are books on the religion of Israel, or on the theology of the Old Testament, they may have sections on this subject.
- Tell this "advocate" that in this week's session, as the story of these three miracles is read, you will expect her or him to interrupt with objections from the point of view of a good, strict religious person of the time of Jesus. He or she is to enact the horror of such a person at what Jesus did and try to get the class to understand those reactions.
- Remind your "advocate" that all Galileans were regarded askance by Jews from Jerusalem, that it was acceptable for that prejudice to come through in his or her interventions. Add that "the country of the Gerasenes" was Gentile territory. Pay special attention to how this person would react to the mention in the stories of Gentiles, tombs, pigs, blood, and a dead girl.

(F) Exercise your imagination.

One of the points made in the study book is that salvation also has a communal dimension. What is suggested here is a way of bringing this to the attention of the class.

- Divide the class into three groups. Assign one of the stories to each group.
- Ask each group to react to the story from the perspective of those who received back the person who had been ill. (For instance, one group may try to imagine the reaction of the brother and sister of the Gerasene demoniac. Another group may try to imagine the reaction of the son of the woman who suffered from hemorrhages. The third group may think about Jairus' wife—the mother of the girl who had died.)
- Tell them that this is an exercise in imagination. They are each to prepare a very short skit in which they tell the rest of the class what happened: how their loved one had been lost, how their loved one was returned, and so forth. They can take hints from the text (for instance, that the demoniac was sometimes restrained with chains). The point they must make is that each of the three had been barred from community and that now the obstacle has been removed.
   Make certain that this dimension of salvation in community comes across in the skits. If it does not, you may wish to bring it out through further questions and discussion.

(G) Discuss salvation.

- Raise the same issues of salvation and community by means of a discussion, leaving out the work in groups and the roleplaying.
- Point out that in each of the three stories the person had been blocked from community. Explain how this was true in each of the three cases. Now make the point that this is one of the aspects of total, integral salvation. Allow opportunity for discussion in case some group members do not agree.

Dimension 3:
What Does the Bible Mean to Us?

(H) Explore the existence of demons.

In the study book, we discussed the matter of "demons." If that is an obstacle for your group that makes it difficult for them to deal with the story of the Gerasene, you may wish to provide opportunity for a discussion on the subject.

- Share the following information:
   The issue regarding demons is not whether there are little ugly things flying around in the air (as we often paint them in cartoons). Such "demons" are actually funny and not very threatening at all. The question is rather whether we must still retain the notion of the "demonic"—of evil which we can neither understand nor control—or whether we can actually dispose of it.
   This is not a question of which is right, science or faith. The fact that we know of physical and chemical causes for mental disorders does not make them any less

demonic. All we have done is push the mystery one step back. The mystery is still just as ominous.
- Discuss:
—Could it be that the reason why we refuse to speak of the demonic is that we are in truth so afraid of it that we would rather make unscientific affirmations about science, which can never explain the reason for evil and for suffering?

(I) Consider what "pulls" at you.

- Share the following information:
   The study book suggests that we should be able to empathize with a man possessed by a demon named "Legion." (A Roman legion had some four to six thousand soldiers. Therefore a "legion" was quite a few!) The point is that we are so divided that we do not know where we are going—nor even where we wish to go—and that in that sense also we are "lost."
- Ask the class:
—Have you ever felt so divided among various goals and responsibilities that you have felt that your very identity was being dissolved among them?
- Share:
   The word *stress*, so commonly used to describe our situation today, in fact refers to the condition of being influenced by various contraposing forces. That seems very similar to what the Gerasene is speaking of when he says that inside himself he is "legion.")
   In contrast to that condition, Soren Kierkegaard said that "purity of heart is to will one thing."
- Discuss these questions:
—Are we willing too many things at once?
—Even worse, are these things contradictory and mutually exclusive?

(J) Extend the discussion.

- List on newsprint or chalkboard the goals toward which class members strive. The list should include both religious goals and others (things such as "greater obedience," "financial security," or "success in a job.")
- Ask:
—Are these goals, in fact, mutually exclusive?

(K) Hold a debate.

The main point of the class is the communal dimension of salvation. This is the reason why we have emphasized that the people whom Jesus healed were not only restored to health, but also restored to the possibility of community.

- Pose the same question, and organize a more formal debate between two teams of two or three members each.
- Set a clear time limit for each participant (for instance, two minutes each). When a debater's time is up, ring a bell or give them some other such sign.

• When all participants in the formal debate have spoken, open the discussion to the rest of the group. (You may restrict discussion only to those who watched the debate.)

> Optional Method: Make this point by a simple discussion of a phrase that appears in the study book: "Faith is also a communal thing."
> —Is this true? Why? Why not?

(L) Simulate our need for community.

• Bring several brooms or mops to class.
• Give one broom or mop to designated participants.
• Ask those participating to try to balance their broom or mop so that it stands on end. (Unless the broom is so scraggly as to be unusable, it cannot be done.)
• Bring participants together in groups of three. Tell them to lean the brooms and/or mops against each other, and they will stand (like a tripod).

This is a basic reality of human life. We cannot be ourselves all alone. To be absolutely solitary, one has to be ill like the Gerasene demoniac. We need each other. We have been made in such a way that we must support each other. What is true of life in general is particularly true of faith.

(M) Look at pictures of "clean and unclean."

The theme of being unclean can be related to those whom our society considers unworthy. Some of these people are mentioned in the study book. There is an obvious connection between being considered "unclean" and being excluded from community. It is important for us to understand that too often our churches and congregations discriminate against those whom society considers unclean.

• Clip from magazines and newspapers a collection of photographs of people. These should be people from various walks of life, involved in different activities, representing a variety of races and ages, of both sexes, dressed in distinct clothes that give some idea of class and/or occupation. Try to have at least three or four such pictures per member of your class.
• Distribute the pictures among the participants. Ask group members to select from them those people whom they might expect to see in your church. Put in a separate stack those whom they would not expect to see.
• Take the two stacks and put them up side by side on a bulletin board or mount them safely on the wall.
• Ask the class if they see any patterns or common characteristics in either of the two groups.
• List responses.

• Lead a discussion regarding the characteristics that mark people whom we would not expect to see in church.
• Ask:
—What can and should we do to correct the situation?

> Optional Method: Collect pictures using the same principles described above, although in fewer numbers—one for each member of the class. Distribute them, one to a participant. Go around the circle, asking each person to show the picture he or she is holding, to say something about what or who the person is, and to say whether she or he believes that this is the sort of person who might come to our church on Sunday. If not, ask why. Conclude with a discussion on what could be done to make our church more inclusive and especially welcoming to those who are not generally welcome in other places.

Additional Bible Helps

Gerasenes, Gadarenes, Gergesenes

Different translations use three names for the people of the region where the man with the demon(s) lived—Gerasenes, Gadarenes, Gergesenes. The reason for this is that in ancient manuscripts the name of the region is spelled in three different ways. No one knows exactly where this locale was, except that obviously it was across the lake from Galilee. The most likely place has the modern name of "Kersa," which may be a variant of one of the names in the ancient manuscripts. It is on the east side of the lake of Galilee. Roughly a mile south of Kersa there is a "steep bank." Although at present there is a distance of about a hundred feet from the bottom of the slope to the lake, in ancient times the lake may have reached further.

The Abyss

The demons begged Jesus not to send them back to "the abyss." In Mark they begged him not to send them far away. There is no exact parallel in Matthew, where they simply begged to be allowed into the swine. The Greek word used here is the same which the ancient Greek translation of the Old Testament used to translate the "deep" of Genesis 1:2. It was primal chaos. It was also the place where monsters lived, according to several passages in the Book of Psalms (see for instance, Psalm 148:7). In the Book of Revelation, it was the "bottomless pit" from whence the beast arose (Revelation 11:7). Apparently, Luke understood the abyss to be the primal chaos, the bottomless pit from which the demons have come and the place where they will be confined in the end.

Note that Jesus agreed to their request, and allowed them to take over a herd of swine. Then, apparently through the action of the demons themselves, the herd threw itself into the sea. So, ironically enough, the demons ended up in the deep waters anyhow.

Fear

The Gerasenes rejected Jesus and asked him to leave. Yet they did not reject him for religious reasons, as did his fellow Jews (at least in Luke, for in John they rejected him for political motives [John 11:45-48]). Rather, they rejected him out of fear. Apparently they were overwhelmed by what had happened. It was not clear whether what caused them to fear was the healing of the man or the death of the pigs. In any case, it was out of fear that they asked him to leave.

Jairus

Jairus was a leader of the synagogue. This did not make him part of the religious elite. Jairus was a leader of the synagogue in far away and despised Galilee. In Luke's work, and especially in the early chapters of Acts, the "people" generally supported Jesus and the early church. It was the leaders—the real elite in Jerusalem—who persecuted and tried to suppress both Jesus and the early church.

The Unclean Woman

It is interesting to note that the woman had been ill for twelve years, and Jairus' daughter was twelve years old. One had been ritually "dead" for twelve years and was then brought back to life. The other has been alive for the same twelve years but now faced death.

The unclean woman had spent all she had on physicians. It is interesting to note that a number of ancient manuscripts do not include this phrase in the Gospel of Luke, although Mark did include the general idea. Could it be that Luke, "the physician," felt that this was an unnecessary slur on his profession? It is an interesting thought.

The Fringe of His Clothes

"Fringe" may simply refer to the hem of Jesus' clothes. The word that Luke used, however, could also mean one of the "fringes" or tassels commanded in Deuteronomy 22:12: "You shall make tassels on the four corners of the cloak with which you cover yourself." The word that Luke used here is the same that appears in Matthew 23:5, where Jesus criticized the Pharisees for making "their fringes long."

Daughter

Note that the same word is used for the two women. Jesus called the woman who has been healed "daughter." The young woman who died and is resurrected is known only as the daughter of Jairus.

All Wept and Wailed

They were all weeping and wailing . . . and they laughed. The subject of the two is the same. Apparently Luke was trying to convey a situation in which these people, who were quite distressed, actually laughed when someone came with what appeared to be too easy a solution to their distress. Strange as it may seem at first, it is a very perceptive description of people's reactions in such extreme situations. In the midst of tragedy, the only way that these people had to express their outrage at what Jesus was suggesting was by laughing.

Tell No One

Jesus ordered the parents of the healed girl to tell no one. Note the contrast between this command and what Jesus told the Gerasene demoniac to do. There has been much debate about what has been called "the Messianic secret" of Jesus. There are many other instances in the Gospel of Luke where Jesus commanded people not to tell who he is or what he had done. Apparently, Jesus was particularly interested in keeping the secret from Jews. That may be why, in the Gentile country of the Gerasenes, he commanded the man to go and tell, whereas here in Galilee he commanded silence.

8

Luke 12:22-48

$\mathcal{P}$REPARING FOR THE FUTURE

LEARNING MENU

Keeping in mind the ways in which your class members learn best as well as their needs and interests, choose at least one learning segment from each of the three Dimensions.

Dimension 1:
What Does the Bible Say?

(A) Answer the questions in the study book.

● Preferably, class members will have read this chapter and answered the questions in Dimension 1 of the study book before the class session. However, some classes may wish to
—share and check their answers together during class;
—discuss their answers as part of the class session;
—work on answering the questions together during class.
Spend the least amount of time necessary in looking at questions and answers in Dimension 1.

(B) Examine Jesus' teachings.

The study book indicates that in this discourse Jesus was addressing his disciples.

● Bring to class a "red-letter" Bible (a Bible that prints the words of Jesus in red.) Hold it up before the class. Point out how little of our passage is in black.

● Note the following:
We are in the midst of a long section in Luke where primarily Jesus speaks. Until last week most of what we studied was narrative *about* Jesus. In these narratives, Jesus was obviously quoted, and sometimes he spoke at some length. This section consists mostly of Jesus' teachings, with brief words of introduction and other comments to connect one passage with the next. In order to demonstrate this fact, you may wish to leaf through the Gospel of Luke in the red-letter Bible, showing the class that in the early chapters most of the print is in black as well as are the chapters near the end of the Gospel. Here, in the section that we are now studying, most of the print is in red, indicating that Jesus himself is speaking. Obviously, this means that while the beginning and the end of the Gospel of Luke deal mostly with the actions of Jesus and of those around him, the middle of the Gospel deals mostly with his teachings.

- Still showing your red-letter Bible, point out that in the entire passage we are studying there are only two brief sections in black—one in verse 22 and the other in verses 41-42. (Both of these serve to clarify Jesus' audience.)
- Read each of these sections so that it becomes clear that in each, Jesus was primarily addressing his disciples. (If you wish, you may also point to the previous section, verses 13-21, where the black-letter sections clearly show that Jesus was in the middle of a multitude, and speaking to them.)

(C) Examine Peter's question.

- Read aloud Peter's question in verse 41.
- Ask:
—Did Jesus answer the question?
—If so, how?

Dimension 2:
What Does the Bible Mean?

(D) Set the stage.

- Set the stage for the entire passage we are studying by briefly retelling what Luke says in verses 13-21. In particular, make certain that the class realizes that the passages we are studying appear immediately after the story about the man who decided to build bigger barns.

(E) Center group attention.

- Center the group's attention on the passage about the birds and the lilies (verses 22-31). State that some people have thought that this means that material things such as food and clothing are not important.
- Ask:
—Is that what the text says? (Allow ample time for discussion, but try to keep the discussion centered on the text.)

   The issue is not whether food and clothing are important. The issue is rather what the text says on the matter. Try to keep the discussion from becoming confrontational, so that someone will win and someone will lose. Rather, tell the class that what you are trying to do is to discover together the meaning of the text. If others do not make the point, you may wish to remind the class that what the text says is that God knows that we need food and clothing, and that therefore we should leave the worrying to God. This is not the same as saying that such things are unimportant. On the contrary, it means that they are so important that God takes care of them!

(F) Highlight the role of food and clothing.

One way of highlighting the significance of food and clothing is by pointing to other places in the Bible where they play a central role. Suggest some of these, and give the class opportunity to suggest others:
—In the story of Creation, we are told that God put humankind in a garden where there were all kinds of plants to eat. Later, also in Genesis, the first thing that God did after expelling Adam and Eve from Eden was to provide them with clothing.
—In the story of the flight from Egypt (the Exodus), when the people were hungry and thirsty, God provided manna, and birds from the sky, and water from the rock.
—In the New Testament, Jesus said that clothing and feeding others was tantamount to clothing and feeding him (Matthew 25:40).

(G) Highlight significant words.

- Highlight the words *do not keep striving* and *strive* in verses 29-31. Note that other versions use the verb *seek*.
- Ask the questions:
—Why do you think Jesus told his disciples not to strive for food or clothing, but to strive rather for the Kingdom?
—Does not the Kingdom include food and clothing? (That is, a situation in which all are fed and clothed?)
In this discussion, one possible conclusion is that we are told not to strive individually for our own food and clothing, because this produces conflict, and often results in injustice. We are to strive rather for the Kingdom, in which—among other things—everyone's needs are met.

(H) Engage in discussion.

- Discuss:
   Jesus said: "Sell your possessions, and give alms. Make purses for yourselves that do not wear out, an unfailing treasure in heaven" (33).
- Ask:
—Was what Jesus saying the same thing as Proverbs 19:17: "Whoever is kind to the poor lends to the Lord, and will be repaid in full"?

(I) Form small groups.

- Divide the class into three groups.
- Assign to each group one of the three parables in verses 35-38; 39; and 41-48. Have group members study their assigned parable for a few minutes, then prepare to present it before the class.
—One way to do this would be simply to tell the story.
—Another way would be to act it out. However, since you

want to make it easy for the class to compare the three stories, give instructions in one direction or another, so that either all three parables are acted out, or all three are simply told.

- While the groups are studying and discussing their parable, and how they are to tell it, write on newsprint or chalkboard the two verses that explain the parables: verses 40 and 48b.
- Bring the class back together and give each group an opportunity to present its parable.
- When presentations are completed, ask the entire group to compare the three stories:

—What are some of the commonalities? (Obviously, all three speak of a master who has gone away. Also, in all three the time of visitation is unknown.)

—What are the differences? (For instance, in the first and third parables the Lord is the master who may come unexpectedly; in the second, the one who comes unexpectedly is a thief. Also, the second parable has no servants or slaves. In the first there are slaves, but no steward, as in the third. The first includes the beautiful promise that the master will become like a servant to his faithful servants. In the first, there is reference to a reward for good behavior, but no reference to a punishment. In the second, there is reference to neither reward nor punishment. In the third, the point is clearly made of both reward for the good steward, and punishment for the bad.)

- Read verse 40.
- Ask:

—Which of the three parables make this point? (The first and second.)

- Read the final section of verse 48, and ask the same question. (This applies quite clearly and directly to the third parable; and also, although not as clearly, to the first.)

Dimension 3:
What Does the Bible Mean to Us?

The passage we are studying, as well as the passage about the man who decided to build bigger barns, challenges many of our contemporary practices and perspectives when it comes to money and financial planning. For this reason, they are often ignored. Yet, that is not a responsible way to deal with Scripture, or with the teachings of Jesus. Therefore, it is important that the class have an opportunity to discuss what these very difficult passages may mean for us today.

(J) Study a concordance.

We have said in the study book that the Gospel of Luke

pays special attention to the poor, as well as to various economic matters.

- Look up in a concordance the words *poor* and *rich* in the Gospel of Luke. (You may find a concordance in such places as local church libraries, public libraries, your pastor's study, and some bookstores.) You will immediately note that Luke uses these words more often than any of the other Gospels writers.
- Record the passages where these words appear on separate pieces of paper.
- Before the class session, put these pieces of paper on the walls, bulletin board, doors, or any other place that is suitable. The idea is to be surrounded by these quotes from Luke.
- Do not say anything about why these quotes have been put up, until you get to this point in the class session.
- Explain that too often we avoid what the Bible says about economic matters. Explain that not discussing these issues is not a proper way of dealing with them.
- Invite reactions from the class to the following questions.

—How do you feel about these various quotes?

—Do you wish they were not in the Bible?

—Do you find them inspiring and edifying?

—Do you find them offensive?

- Ask a further question:

Apparently, the Theophilus to whom the Gospel of Luke was addressed was fairly well-to-do—at least Luke addresses him as "most excellent Theophilus," a treatment reserved for people who were fairly high on the social scale.

—How do you think Theophilus would react to these various passages?

—Would Luke have had a greater chance of a fair hearing if he had not included these various sayings about the poor and the rich?

—Why do you think Luke included them?

—How does our own social standing affect the way we react to these texts?

—Are we fairly well-to-do? Are we poor?

—Would we react differently if we were at one or another extreme of the social and economic scale?

(K) Consider anxiety.

- Read aloud verses 22-34.
- Ask:

—Does this mean that we should not buy insurance, or try to build equity, or plan for retirement?

Allow sufficient time for a discussion in which all feel free to express their opinions. These opinions may vary. What follows are some possible answers that other discussion groups on the same subject have suggested. You may wish to try some of them with your group, and see if they find them acceptable or helpful:

—Pension systems, insurance companies, and the like are precisely part of what God provides so that we need not be anxious about these things. For us today, what this text means is precisely that we should make use of these means, in order not to be anxious.

—These words were addressed to a simpler society where there was no way to make provision for the future. They are not really meant for us.

The entire passage is to be read in the light of what Jesus said about striving for the Kingdom. The problem with being "anxious" is not just what that anxiety does to us. Jesus was not saying these words as a clue to our personal tranquility and happiness, like a pop psychologist who tells us that anxiety is bad. It is also that when we are overly anxious about the future, and try to build our own security with excessive zeal, we tend to become greedy and callous. When our anxiety leads us to hoard things and money to such an extent that others suffer, we are working against the Kingdom. In the final analysis, the measure is not whether we are anxious or not; the measure is whether we are serving the Kingdom or impeding it.

(L) Explore the meaning of righteousness.

The text we are studying is oriented toward the future. In particular, it is oriented toward the reign or kingdom of God and toward the return of Jesus.

● Share the following information:

—Although we often think that what determines our actions is in the past, there is also a very important role for the future. When we send our children to school, we do so because we envision a future in which what they learn today at school will be valuable. When in school we usually decide on a particular major in view of a future for which we hope—a future as a teacher, as a physical therapist, as a law enforcement officer, as a landscape designer, as a pastor, and so forth. Even when it comes to smaller elements in life, the future helps determine our actions. For instance, when I come out of my driveway and decide whether to turn left or right, I do so on the basis of where I am going—in other words, of where I envision myself in the near future. As I write these lines, I choose my words while trying to envision a future occasion when you will be reading them. And as you read them, you are thinking about what to do with them in the class session that will take place in the near future.

That is the connection between the three parables and the earlier part of the text. The three parables refer to the future that we as Christians expect and await. The earlier part of the text says that we ought to strive, not primarily for the security of food and clothing, but for the security of the Kingdom. The text says that people who really believe in the promised reign of God will live accordingly.

● Offer the class an example:

—Suppose I were to tell you that I believe Japan is the most beautiful country in the world, and that I can hardly wait until I retire so that I can move to Japan. There is no place like Japan. There is no food like Japanese food. There is no art like Japanese art. There is no place where I would rather be than in Japan. I can hardly wait!

—Suppose further that you then say to me: "That is very exciting. What are you doing while you wait for retirement and can move to Japan?"

—Suppose that my answer is: "Oh, I am studying Italian."

—At this point, the class will probably laugh! There is an incongruence between my actions and my avowed hope and expectation. It is an incongruence that is both comic and tragic, for either I am wasting my time now learning Italian, or I will not be very comfortable when I finally move to Japan. If I really mean all that I am saying about Japan, I had better begin studying Japanese or two things will happen: First, no one will believe my witness about Japan. Second, when the day arrives for me to move to Japan, I will not be ready.

● Ask the class:

—What happens when we spend so much time speaking about the coming reign of God, when we even pray daily, "Your Kingdom come," but do not take the trouble to begin to learn "kingdomese"?

—Will people believe us? Will we believe ourselves?

—Could this be one of the reasons why some people are so ready to ignore the witness of the church?

—How can we begin practicing "kingdomese" here and now?

—How can we begin acting like the steward who really believes that the master will come and require an account?

—What would acting like the steward mean in terms of our economic life, since at least part of the text deals with that?

● End the class by reading again one or more of the parables in the text, depending on how much time remains.

Additional Bible Helps

Do Not Keep Striving

"Do not keep striving" (verse 29) translates a Greek word that could literally be translated as "do not be up on the air." The image here is not of one who keeps striving like an athlete, running on a set course. It is rather of one whose anxiety is flighty, never resting on anything solid, preventing real or effective action.

The "Proper" Allowance

In verse 42, we are told that the steward has been put in charge of the other slaves, "to give them their allowance of food at the proper time." The word that the NRSV Bible translates as "allowance of food" is a rather technical term which means "measure of grain." This immediately brings to mind several other passages in the Bible that refer to the same notion:

- In Exodus 16:16-18, there is an aspect of the miracle of the manna that we often forget. Moses instructed the people to gather only a measure of manna per member of a household. The people did not obey, with the result that some gathered too much, and some were not able to gather enough. When they measured what they had gathered, they found that each had the right amount— neither too much, nor too little.
- The same idea appears in Proverbs 30:8: "Feed me with the food that I need." You may wish to read the entire passage, Proverbs 30:7-9. What the poet is asking for is the exact right amount—neither too much nor too little —for either too much or too little would be bad.
- In the Lord's Prayer, we use practically the same phrase when we say "give us this day our daily bread."
- In 2 Corinthians 8:15, Paul refers to the miracle of the redistribution of the manna as a basis for the collection for the poor in Jerusalem. (Again, you may wish to read the entire passage, 2 Corinthians 8:8-15.) His point is that the church should reenact that miracle in its own life.

What all this means is that the task of the steward, "to give them their allowance of food at their proper time," is closely connected with the biblical notion of God's action, and with Paul's understanding of how the church is to imitate what God did with the manna. A steward gives the other slaves "their allowance of food at the proper times," because that is how the master is.

Quotes on Luke's Themes of Fear and Possessions

Luke's bringing together of the two themes (fear and possessions) shows how profoundly he has grasped the symbolic function of possessions in human existence. It is out of deep fear that the acquisitive instinct grows monstrous. Life seems so frail and contingent that many possessions are required to secure it, even though the possessions are frailer still than the life. Only the removal of fear by the persuasion that life is a gift given by the source of all reality can generate the spiritual freedom. . . . (*The Gospel of Luke*, by Luke T. Johnson, Liturgical Press, 1991; page 201)

The one with the most toys when he dies, wins. (A bumper sticker seen on the road.)

Greed is the cause of our want. The birds have abundant food because they have received in common that which is necessary for their nourishment, and they do not know how to claim private ownership. . . . Birds, who own nothing, lack nothing. (St. Ambrose, Bishop of Milan)

What is a miser? One who is not content with what is needful. What is a thief? One who takes what belongs to others. Why do you not consider yourself a miser and a thief when you claim as your own what you received in trust? If one who takes the clothing off another is considered a thief, why give any other name to one who can clothe the naked and refuses to do so? (St. Basil, Bishop of Caesarea)

Wealth is not a possession, it is not property, it is a loan for use. For when thou diest, willingly or unwillingly, all that thou hast goes to others, and they again give it up to others, and they again to others. Goods . . . are not our own, and possessions are not a property but a loan. For how many masters has every estate had, and how many more will it have! (St. John Chrysostom, Bishop of Constantinople)

As to yourself, you are not the proprietor of any thing; no, not of one shilling in the world. You are only a steward of what another entrusts you with, to be laid out, not according to your will, but his. (John Wesley)

Therefore, every shilling which you needlessly spend on your apparel is, in effect, stolen from God and the poor! (John Wesley)

9

Luke 13:1-9

THE PARABLE OF THE FIG TREE

LEARNING MENU

Again, keeping in mind the ways in which your class members learn best, as well as their needs and interests, choose at least one learning segment from each of the three Dimensions.

Dimension 1: What Does the Bible Say?

The answers to questions raised in the study book are best grappled with in activity (D). For this session, do not spend time answering those very questions as your session begins but rather hold that discussion until later.

(A) Connect two parts of the text.

● Read verses 1-5 aloud.
● Ask:
—Do any themes or actual words appear more than once in these verses? (The theme of unexpected and apparently unmerited death, while others live, appears both in reference to the incident with the Galileans and in reference to the tower. Also, the words "unless you repent, you will all perish" appear at the end of Jesus' words on each of these two incidents.)

● Read the parable of the barren fig tree (6-9).
● Ask:
—Do you see any of these themes repeated or alluded to in the parable? (The theme of repentance is alluded to in the fruit that the owner wants. The theme of dying unless you repent appears in the final instructions: "If it bears fruit next year, well and good; but if not, you can cut it down." The theme of some dying while others live appears in the contrast between a repeatedly pruned vineyard, and a verdant fig tree. However, since this is not as clear, you may wish to let this go unmentioned until further along in the session.)

(B) Invite initial reactions to the text.

● Ask class members for initial reactions to the text.
—Did they see the point?
—Were they baffled by it?
—Did they see any connection between the first and second parts of the passage?
—Did the parable make any sense?
If you follow this option, keep in mind that this is not the point to try to respond to doubts or problems that participants may have had in their initial reading. That is the agenda of the rest of the session. What you wish to do here is simply to take the pulse of the class, to see whether they reacted to the reading with a sense of puzzlement, as most readers do. Your purpose is also to show that such a sense

of puzzlement is acceptable and quite common. As you study the text with more care in the rest of the lesson, hopefully this will also serve as an example of how much of our puzzlement can be solved by simply reading a text carefully.

Dimension 2:
What Does the Bible Mean?

(C) Reflect on Luke's context.

Since in their Daily Bible Journey Plan the participants will already have read through this passage, you may wish to take some time to place it in its context in the whole narrative of Luke. We have just passed the mid-point in the Gospel.

● Review what they have read with a series of questions such as:
—Has Jesus already announced his death?
—Is he on his way to Jerusalem? (Again, using a red-letter Bible, you may show that, in general, there is more black type than red up to and through chapter 9. Chapter 9 is a turning point in that there Luke tells the reader who Jesus really is and what his mission is. Note that in that chapter you have the confession of Peter, the Transfiguration, and the famous saying that Jesus "set his face to go to Jerusalem." Then, beginning in chapter 10, Luke clarifies Jesus' teachings, using Jesus himself as the main speaker. It is in this section that Luke concentrates the parables of Jesus, and many of his other sayings. Finally, in chapter 19, with Jesus' arrival at Jerusalem, black type becomes dominant again. In other words, we are back to narratives about Jesus again with some of his words and teachings interspersed. In this section that we are studying, the "action" is slow, but the teaching is constant.)
—How many parables are there in chapter 12? (Remember last week's session.)
—What are some of the points they make?

(D) Analyze the text.

Lead the class in an analysis of the first five verses, as follows:
● Divide the chalkboard or newsprint into three columns. Put a heading above each of the columns labeled "victims," "cause," and "survivors." (See the example at the top of the next column.)
● Read verses 1-3 aloud.
● Ask the class these questions:
—Who were the victims? (Obviously, the dead Galileans.)
—Who or what caused their suffering? (Pilate.)
—Who is mentioned as survivors?

● Write the answers in each column, so that at this point you will have something like:

Victims	Cause	Survivors
Some Galileans	Pilate	All other Galileans

● Point out some of the difficult political implications of the conversation in which Jesus was engaged. (Galileans were generally considered as inferior Jews, whose faith was somehow contaminated. Pilate was the all-powerful Roman governor. Jesus, himself a Galilean, was going toward Jerusalem with his Galilean disciples.) This setting merits some discussion.
● Read verses 4-5 aloud.
● Ask:
—Who were the victims? (the eighteen on whom the tower fell) Who or what was the cause? (the tower that fell) Who were the survivors? (all the rest who were living in Jerusalem)
● As the group considers answers to these questions, add another line to each column, as follows:

Victims	Cause	Survivors
Some Galileans	Pilate	All other Galileans
18 Jews	Tower	Others in Jerusalem

● Broaden the discussion by bringing out some of the other dimensions of the text. (Note that Jesus changed the tone and context of the conversation at several points.)
—Jesus moved the discussion from the senseless death of some Galileans to the equally senseless death of eighteen people in Jerusalem. Without explicitly saying anything about that, Jesus disarmed those whose prejudice would lead them to say that these Galileans were killed because, not being good Jews, they should not have been offering sacrifices. In other words, Jesus was avoiding the easy pitfall of blaming the victim.
—By talking about an incident in which a tower fell, apparently through no one's fault that could be determined, Jesus was both simplifying the question and making it more difficult. He simplified it by moving it away from the difficult arena of politics and nationalism. The incident of the Galileans brought to the fore all kinds of issues of politics, nationalism, regionalism, and so forth. In that sense, by speaking about the tower of Siloam, Jesus simplified the question. At the same time he made it more difficult, for the problem that was now posed was that some people did suffer utterly senseless deaths. In the case of the Galileans, at least there was Pilate to blame. In the case of the tower there was no one.

44

—By asking if those who died when the tower fell were "worse offenders than all the others living in Jerusalem" (4), Jesus brought into question the view that Jerusalem was a center of holiness, and that on the basis of that holiness, people there would receive a special treatment from God. Those people living in Jerusalem on whom the tower did not fall were as sinful as those whom the tower killed.

—Finally, note that Jesus ended his remarks about each of the two incidents with the same words, to the effect that all would perish unless they repented—the Galileans who survived, the people in Jerusalem who also survived, and "you," meaning his entire audience.

(E) Consider the fig tree.

● Read verses 6-9 aloud. Your purpose is to show the connection between this parable and the preceding words of Jesus.

● Invite the class to retell what their books say about how vines are pruned and about this fig tree not having been pruned.

● Ask:

—Can you describe how this fig tree and this vineyard would look to a casual observer who knew nothing about the cultivation of vineyards or about fig trees? How would it look to someone looking for fruit at the last possible chance, say in the early fall? (This has been explained in the study book. All that would be left of the vines would be some rather gnarled remains, heavily pruned. The fig tree would still be green and growing unencumbered.)

● Go back to the chart created for activity (D).

● Ask:

—What would a casual observer put under each of the columns? (You will probably end up with something like the following:

Victims	Cause	Survivors
Some Galileans	Pilate	Some other Galileans
18 Jews	Tower	Others in Jerusalem
Vines	Vinedresser (or owner)	Fig tree

—Suppose you knew that the fig tree had produced no fruit. How could you explain the situation? (Basically, two answers are possible. Either the vinedresser and the owner of the vineyard are grossly unfair, or they are giving the fig tree another chance to bear fruit. The latter is the explanation that Jesus gives in the biblical text.)

● End this entire section by making sure that all participants now understand the connection between verses 1-5

on the one hand, and verses 6-9 on the other. If they do, the point of the parable should be clear.

Dimension 3:
What Does the Bible Mean to Us?

There are two main issues that must be dealt with as we study this text: the question of apparently senseless suffering and the "gospel of success."

(F) Refer to contemporary events.

Consider the question of suffering. There is a widespread notion that suffering is always punishment for the sins of the person who suffers. This results in two very serious consequences:

(1) When people who are distant from us suffer, it is very easy to blame them for their own suffering. That is often called "blaming the victim."

(2) When we ourselves or a loved one suffer, we tend to blame ourselves for it, and this in turn makes the suffering doubly painful.

● To bring this text to bear on these issues, ask the class to rewrite verses 1-5 as they refer to contemporary events. For the Galileans, substitute some contemporary, suffering group that is relatively distant from the class and its experience. For the people whom the tower killed, substitute another example that is much closer to home.

● Ask:

—What does this tell us about why some people suffer and others do not—or about why some people suffer more than others? (In the final analysis, what makes suffering so painful is precisely the fact that it does not make sense. By definition, there is no final answer to the question of suffering. All we can say is that it is wrong to think that when someone suffers it must be a punishment for a specific sin that person has committed.)

(G) Explore the gospel of success.

The other subject with which we must deal in this context is the "gospel of success." Repeatedly, Christians are told that God rewards with material goods or other signs of "success" for their faithfulness. In recent years, there have been famous preachers whose measure of faithfulness was that God gave them gold faucets for their bathrooms and expensive cars to drive. The text we are studying clearly has something to say on that issue.

● Ask the class the following questions:

—Can you think of any people who are or were like vines that had been pruned—people whose faithfulness to God is or was exemplary, and yet they suffered?

—Can you think of persons who showed their faithfulness in the way they responded to difficulties in their lives? (These may be personal friends, acquaintances, or historical figures. It is important to have opportunities for this kind of testimonial in our Christian circles. Christians need to hear that there are indeed people whose success consists not in having many things, nor in being famous or powerful, but in being faithful servants of God and others.)

• As the conversation progresses, list some of the names on the chalkboard or newsprint where you had your three columns (as in activity (D). List names in the "victims" column. List people who, to a casual observer of society, would look like vines unjustly pruned, suffering more than their due, while "fruitless fig trees" continued to prosper.

(H) Remember those whom society calls successful.

• Add to the chart developed in activity (D). Under the column heading "survivors," write categories of people whom our society tends to think are particularly successful—music superstars, sports heroes, highly prosperous entrepreneurs, powerful politicians.

• List, with the aid of class members, some of the "successful" people of Jesus' time (people such as Pilate, the High Priest, or the Roman Emperor.) List in the column labeled "fig tree" these identified persons on the chart from activity (D).

• Ask:
—Where does Jesus fall in this chart?

• With big letters in the column that includes the "victims," write "JESUS."

• In this connection, read aloud Isaiah 53.
—How closely does this description of the suffering servant of God resemble the sufferings of Jesus?
—How closely does this description of the suffering servant of God resemble the pruning of a vine? (If there is no time to read Isaiah 53 in class, suggest that participants read it later at home, while reflecting on the learnings of this lesson.)

• Remind the class that Luke wrote a sequel to his Gospel and that in that sequel, the Book of Acts, he will repeatedly show the church being "pruned" and yet bearing ever more fruit.

(I) Discuss the meaning of the parable for our lives.

Ask some of the following questions:
—What are the things of which we are proud as a congregation? (You may make this question more specific by asking, "When we talk about our church to others, what are the things we boast of?")

—How many of these things are more befitting to fruitful vines, that are pruned precisely so that they can bear more fruit?
—How many are more befitting to fruitless fig trees, that receive special care precisely because they would never bear fruit otherwise?
—In other words, which things of which we boast are the things of which Jesus would have us boast?
—Which are simply things that we think are important because they give us prestige and make us look good?

Additional Bible Helps

Jesus Was on His Way

The phrase "at that very time," may be taken to mean the very time when Jesus was speaking to the crowds at the end of chapter 12. It may also mean the very time when the incident of the Galileans took place, thus indicating that Jesus knew practically immediately what had happened. If so, it was clearly a dire warning against his going to Jerusalem.

The text does not tell us who it was among those present who told Jesus of the incident involving the Galileans. In any case, there is another dimension here that has not been highlighted in the lesson itself, but which adds greater drama to the situation. Remember that Jesus was on his way to Jerusalem. Apparently some travelers coming back from Jerusalem brought the gruesome tale of what had happened to these Galileans. Since Jesus was clearly on his way to Jerusalem, this tale may have been brought to him as a warning of what might have happened to him at the capital. (Remember that in Acts Paul also received warnings of what would happen to him in Jerusalem and decided to go anyhow.) If so, Jesus' answer, and the story of the fig tree, become even more dramatic. Jesus knew that he was about to be "pruned." He foretold it, and now he received direct warning of what had happened to other Galileans in Jerusalem. Thus, his reply was not just a general discussion about suffering and bearing fruit; it was rather an expression of how he saw himself suffering and mocked, while the powerful persons gloated, and many of the people shook their heads in pity.

Pilate and Galilee

Ancient historians have left no record of either of the events to which the text refers: the killing of the Galileans, or the fall of the tower of Siloam.

The episode of the Galileans and Pilate, however, is quite typical of what we know of both Pilate and his relations with Galilee. The Galileans were particularly prone to rebel against Roman rule. We have records of several such rebellions. It is quite possible that when a group of Galileans came to Jerusalem to offer sacrifices, Pilate feared that they were plotting sedition—which they may or may not have been. In that case, Pilate would order them killed. This would be quite consistent with what we know of Pilate's irascible cruelty, especially against those who questioned his authority. The Jewish historian Josephus does not tell of this particular incident; but he does mention others like it. It was a massacre of Samaritans on Mount Gerizim that finally brought about Pilate's recall by the Roman government in A.D. 36. Since Mount Gerizim was the place where the Samaritans worshiped, this incident was very similar to the one told in our story, where a group of Galileans were killed at their place of worship.

The mingling of their blood with their sacrifices, if taken literally, would mean, as suggested in the study book, that they were killed in the Temple itself. However, it may also be a metaphor expressing the deep anger of those who reported the incident. The Galileans went to Jerusalem to spill the blood of sacrifices, and their own blood was also spilled.

Later on in Luke 23:12, Luke will tell us that there had been enmity between Pilate and Herod Antipas, Tetrarch of Galilee. Perhaps there was a connection between that enmity and this incident. It is impossible to tell.

A similar situation existed with reference to the tower of Siloam. This is the only place where that tower or this particular incident are mentioned. We do know that there was a "pool of Siloam," and that one of the ancient Temple walls was close to that pool. The word that the NRSV translates as "tower" refers to the sort of tower that would be found on a wall. Therefore, the incident may have involved a tower within the ancient Temple walls. If so, the relationship with the other incident, which was also connected with the Temple, becomes even closer.

More Stories

There are many ancient stories and proverbs that are reminiscent of the parable of the barren fig tree. Perhaps the closest is a story in which a palm tree, whose fruit had always fallen into a river, is about to be cut. The palm tree asks for a year of grace and promises its owner to bear carob. The owner rightly responds that a tree that has not even given the fruit to be expected of it is much less likely to give a different kind of fruit. (This is told in the *Story of Ahikar*, an ancient Jewish book probably written around the year 200 B.C.)

The fig tree and the vine are mentioned together in the Bible in more than one place. See, for instance, Joel 2:22 and Micah 4:4. This is not surprising, since figs and grapes, together with olives, were the most commonly grown fruits in the area at the time.

Although one should not make too much of it, it is interesting to note that what the vinedresser gives the tree so that it will bear fruit is manure! Likewise, many of the so-called "blessings" that we receive precisely so that we may bear fruit, are just so much manure. It is up to us whether to turn them into fruit or into showy, but useless leafy growth.

10

Luke
15:1–32

LOST
AND FOUND

LEARNING MENU

Keeping in mind the ways in which your class members learn best, as well as their needs and interests, choose at least one learning segment from each of the three Dimensions. Use learning segment (A) as class members arrive.

Dimension 1:
What Does the Bible Say?

(A) Answer the questions from the study book.

● Encourage early arriving students to compare answers to the questions in the study book, page 77. If class members have not taken the time to answer these questions or to read the content of the study book for this session, provide a few quiet moments for them to do so. Answers for these questions are as follows:

1. Jesus spoke to Pharisees and scribes, defending his ministry to "sinners."

2. Each parable speaks of God's love for the lost.

3. The Pharisees and scribes, the audience for the telling

of these parables, regarded some persons as outside God's concern. These parables remind the religious elite that God is greatly concerned for those the audience considers "lost."

4. Each parable speaks of a particular item that has been lost, animate or inanimate. However there is a commonality to these parables in that God greatly rejoices over the "lost," which is found.

● Spend as little time as possible with learning segment (A), since the "meat" of the passage can be discovered in subsequent activities.

(B) Read the text.

● Invite a class member to read aloud Luke 15:1-32.

(C) Establish the setting for the parables.

● Invite a class member to read aloud the very last sentence of chapter 14 and yet another member to read aloud 15:1.

● Ask:

—Is there any connection between the two?

—Is there a verb that appears in both the last sentence in chapter 14 and the first sentence in chapter 15? (The word *listen* appears in both.)

48

- Point out that Luke presented these tax collectors and sinners in chapter 15 as doing precisely what Jesus had challenged all to do at the end of 14: "Let anyone with ears to hear listen!" The sinners and tax collectors listened, while the Pharisees and the scribes grumbled.
- Ask the class to identify the following:
—Who was around when Jesus told these parables? (Clearly, Luke described these people in two doublets: "tax collectors and sinners" and "the Pharisees and the scribes."
—What do you recall about each of these groups?
—Who were the scribes?
—Who were the Pharisees?
—Who were the tax collectors?
—Who were classified as "sinners"? (Very often those who were called "sinners" were simply people who were too poor to obey and follow all the rituals that the more religious demanded. Sacrifices and special festivals required resources that many of the poorer Jews could not afford. Therefore, they were considered "sinners," because they had not been properly purified.)
—Do you remember other places in the Gospel of Luke where the same sort of people, who were now grumbling, criticized Jesus for the company he kept? (Recall in lesson four where Jesus was invited to eat at the house of Levi, and the Pharisees and their scribes complained to his disciples about the company he was keeping. Remember also lesson 6 where Simon the Pharisee secretly criticized Jesus for allowing a sinful woman to touch him. Obviously, one of the main points of contention between Jesus and the Pharisees and scribes was his openness to welcome people whom the more religious elements in society despised.)

Dimension 2:
What Does the Bible Mean?

(D) Experience the feelings of key players.

- Divide the class into four groups: (1) publicans (tax collectors); (2) sinners; (3) Pharisees; and (4) scribes. Give each group two or three minutes to discuss among themselves, and make sure that they all understand who their characters were in Bible times.
- Ask the Pharisees:
—From your perspective as Pharisees, who among all these people do you consider to be lost? Why?
- Ask the same question of the scribes.
- Tell the publicans and sinners that they know they are lost. They have been told that by every religious leader since they were born. They know that they are not pure,

that their obedience to the law of God leaves much to be desired.
- Place an empty chair at one end of the room. Ask people to imagine that Jesus is sitting there and teaching. Instruct the tax collectors and the sinners to move to that end of the room and crowd around the chair.
- Ask the Pharisees and the scribes:
—What do you think about Jesus' teachings?
- Respond to the scribes and Pharisees by reading the two parables of the lost sheep (15:4-7) and the lost coin (15:8-10).
- Ask the members playing the key roles:
—How did you feel when you heard these parables? (Allow time for discussion and airing of feelings but try to keep each person in his or her proper role, as assigned.)
Follow this activity with either learning segment (E) or (F).

(E) Discover common elements among the parables.

- Invite three people to read the three parables, each person reading one parable.
- Ask:
—What is there in common among all three of these parables?
- List answers on chalkboard or newsprint. If students do not mention the following, share them yourself.
—Something was lost, and then found (a sheep, a coin, a son).
—Something similar was never lost (the ninety-nine sheep, the nine coins, the elder son).
—When the lost is found, there is a great celebration!
- Ask:
—Does this respond to the grumbling of the Pharisees and the scribes? How?
(Follow this activity with learning segment (F).

(F) Read about the "prodigal son."

- Invite a class member to read aloud the parable of the prodigal son (as it has traditionally been called).
- Begin by asking the following questions:
—Are there common themes that appear in this parable, that appear also in the other two? (Obviously, if you used the activity above, you may skip this question, which will already have been discussed.)
—What does this parable add that the other two do not include? (Obviously, there are all kinds of details that have to do with the specific subject of this parable, and which therefore do not appear in the others. Note that up to verse 24 the parable is generally parallel to the other two. Here again, something was lost, and then found—a son; something similar was never lost—the elder son; and when the lost was found, there was a great celebration.

In spite of all the details about the son's going to a distant country and taking care of pigs, the structure of the story is the same. But in verse 25 a new element is introduced: the elder son did not like what was happening. For obvious reasons, in the previous two parables there was no protest from either the ninety-nine sheep or the nine coins that were never lost. But here there was a vigorous and even angry protest from the son who was never lost. Indeed, the protest was such that he risked being alienated from the father, thus becoming "lost.")

● Having made this clear, ask the Pharisees and the publicans:
—You who were grumbling because Jesus welcomed sinners and ate with them, do you now see the point of the parable?

(G) Compare the three parables.

Make the same comparison among the three parables by means of a graphic presentation on the chalkboard or newsprint.
● On the left-hand side of the chart, write headings for three horizontal columns: "Parable 1," "Parable 2," and "Parable 3."
● Across the top of the page, write three other headings for vertical columns: "Lost and Found," "Not Lost," and "Result."
● As a class member reads aloud the first parable, write across the chart one or two corresponding words. Thus, at the end of that reading, you should have something that looks like the following:

	Lost & Found	Not Lost	Result
Parable 1	sheep	99 sheep	celebration

● Invite another class member to read the second parable, following the same procedure:

	Lost & Found	Not Lost	Result
Parable 1	sheep	99 sheep	celebration
Parable 2	coin	9 coins	celebration

● Invite a third member to read the third parable, following the same procedure. All will be simple and fairly similar, until you get to verse 25. Here you will have to add one more dimension to your summary of the parable:

	Lost & Found	Not Lost	Result
Parable 1	sheep	99 sheep	celebration
Parable 2	coin	9 coins	celebration
Parable 3	younger son	elder son	celebration/ protest

● Lead the class in a discussion, using this question as a discussion starter:
—Why do you think that Jesus added this new element in this last parable? (Remember that Jesus was responding to the grumbling of the Pharisees and scribes, precisely the people who would identify with the older son.)

Dimension 3: What Does the Bible Mean to Us?:

In the study book, we suggested the possibility of placing ourselves in different roles in the parables. This is a valuable tool when reading any narrative material, for by changing the person with whom we identify, we gain new insights into the meaning of the narrative. In the case of parables such as these, it is particularly useful, for it keeps us from always identifying at the place that is less challenging or more comfortable.

Thus, the various options that follow are different ways of reading the parables, but it is hoped that you will help the class read the parables from all of these perspectives, and not simply choose one.

(H) Identify with those who are lost.

● Sing the hymn "Amazing Grace" (No. 378, *The United Methodist Hymnal*).
● Ask these questions:
—Do you ever feel that you were lost, and have been found?
—Does anyone wish to share a testimonial of how this has been true in their lives? (Do not shy away from testimonials. We often complain that our churches are not evangelistic enough, and then curtail people who are ready to give witness of what the gospel has meant for them.)
—Was there a point at which, for whatever reason, you felt unworthy, and this parable gave you a sense of worth, of being accepted, of being redeemable?

(I) Identify with those who were not lost.

● Encourage class members to try to identify with one of the ninety-nine sheep that did not go astray, with one of the nine coins that were not lost, or, most especially, with the faithful and obedient son who stayed home.
—How would we feel about the lost being brought in on an equal footing, and with as much fanfare as the younger son who had squandered part of his father's wealth?
—Can we understand the son who did not wish to join the celebration?
—Is there something in us that would cause us to react in the same way?

—Is there any sort of person we do not want in our church?

—If, as the study book says, we are today's scribes and Pharisees, (and remember, being a scribe or a Pharisee was a rather respectable thing), who are the "sinners" and "tax collectors" of our day?

—Who are the people whose presence would make us feel that the church has been disgraced, that we might lose our prestige in the community, that we ourselves are uncomfortable?

—What do the parables say about such people?

—More specifically, what does the parable of the two sons say about us if we begrudge God's grace for them?

Optional Method: Make the same points, and then ask the class to do three things:

—First rewrite the story of the two sons in contemporary terms, using a modern cast of characters. (Class members do not necessarily need to record the story; they may simply brainstorm as to how the story would look in a modern setting.) In this method, discuss who would be today's sinners and tax collectors. Be as specific as possible, placing the parable in your own community and congregation.

—Second, give the parable as it appears in Luke a "happy ending." (For instance, "the older son recognized that his father was right. He went into the house and . . . .")

—Third, suggest what that happy ending would be in the contemporary situation class members portrayed in the first activity above. If in that situation we are the elder son, what would be a "happy ending" for us?

(J) Identify with the one who seeks the lost.

With care not to think that we are God, it is also possible to identify with the one who seeks the lost—the owner of the hundred sheep, the woman with the ten coins, or the father with the two sons. In a way, that is what was required of the older son who did not want to join the celebration. By refusing to enter and to accept his brother, the elder son did not only reaffirm his alienation from his brother; he also alienated himself from the father.

● Read aloud the conversation between the father and this older son in Luke 15:25-32.

● Help the class to understand the following points of the parable.

The father tried to make the son see things as he saw them. Otherwise, he would have been quite justified in his complaint. The father was insistant: This son of mine, your brother, was lost! I must rejoice. Come and rejoice with me! The only way that the son could avoid being alienated from his forgiving and accepting father was also to learn how to forgive and to accept.

What this means is that, if we are to be loving children of God, and not alienated from God, we must learn to forgive and to accept just as God forgives and accepts.

As religious people who are trying to study the Bible and to live under its guidance, we are much closer to the Pharisees and the scribes than to the sinners and tax collectors. They were the religious people of their time. We are the religious people of our time. What Jesus demanded of the Pharisees was not that they cease their efforts at obedience. What Jesus demanded was that they be open to the God who brings outsiders in, who forgives and welcomes the lost sinner. Jesus did not call the Pharisees to become tax collectors, or the scribes to become sinners. He called them to be like the God whom they loved and served: loving, forgiving, accepting.

Likewise, Jesus does not call Christians to become sinners, or to abandon their high standards. Jesus does require Christians to call others to faith and forgiveness.

(K) Discuss evangelism.

Conclude the class with a discussion on evangelism.

● Begin that discussion by sharing the following information in a "mini-lecture."

One of the things that we hear most often is that our churches are not sufficiently evangelistic, and that therefore membership is declining. We are also told that there are millions out there who need to hear the gospel, who are lost, dying in sin, and whom we must invite to come in.

All of these points are true, and unless we as a church recover the urgency to communicate the good news of Jesus Christ, we do not have much reason to continue existing.

There is another dimension that makes the challenge even more serious. Paradoxically, if we do not invite sinners in, we ourselves are left out!

That is the situation in which the older son found himself. If he insisted that his younger brother did not belong in the celebration, he himself would be left out! The father was who he was. The older son's complaints would not change him. The party would go on whether the older son wished it or not. His only options were to join the party by accepting the return of the prodigal or to be left out altogether.

That is the situation in which the Pharisees found themselves. If they insisted that they were not sinners, they would be like the healthy, who had no need of the Divine Physician (remember lesson four). If they insisted in not joining Jesus' celebration of life and forgiveness, they would be left out. Their only options, like the older son's, were to accept Jesus and along with him the sinners and tax collectors, or to stay out of the celebration altogether.

That is the situation in which we, the religious of today, find ourselves. The shepherd is still looking tenderly after the hundredth sheep. The woman is still rejoicing over her tenth coin. The father is still holding a celebration for the prodigal who has returned. We may not like it—we who would like to think that for the most part we have been as obedient as the elder son, as accountable as the nine coins in the woman's purse, as faithful as the ninety-nine sheep. But we have no other options. We either join God's celebration of acceptance and forgiveness, eating, like Jesus, with sinners and tax collectors, or we stand outside and protest, like the elder son.

In short, we need more evangelism. But we need real, drastic evangelism: evangelism that is good news for all who are outside. We need it for them. And we need it for us!

● Allow sufficient time for class members to digest the "mini-lecture" and to discuss their own viewpoints on the importance of evangelism. Resist the temptation to lecture without allowing for discussion time.

Additional Bible Helps

A Connection to Moses and the Wilderness

In verse 2 of this passage, the word that the NRSV translates as "grumbling" is the same Greek word that the ancient Greek version used to translate the "complaining" of the Israelites against Moses. (See Exodus 16:2.) A reader familiar with the Old Testament that most Jews throughout the Empire read at the time, which was this Greek translation, would make a connection between the complaints of the children of Israel in the wilderness and the attitude of the Pharisees and scribes vis-a-vis Jesus. Naturally, this would also bring to mind images of Jesus as the new Moses.

Of Particular Interest to Luke

You may also wish to note that only the first of these three parables has a parallel in any of the other Gospels (Matthew 18:12-14). Even there, the point that the parable makes is somewhat different. The emphasis on the lost and the found, so nicely woven together in these three parables, appears only in Luke.

Drachmas

The coins that the woman had, which the NRSV translates as "silver coins," were *drachmas*, each worth approximately one day's wage. Thus, this woman was not rich, although neither was she destitute.

The Parable of the Two Sons

There are a number of details in the parable of the two sons that may be worth noting:

(1) The younger son's act of asking for his share of "the property that will belong to me" was, in fact, an insult to the father. His crime was not just that he left. His crime was also that he acted as though he wished that his father were dead by asking for his inheritance ahead of time.

(2) Note that in verse 12 the father "divided the property between them." Yet, at the end of the story the father is still the owner and manager of the remaining portion, to the point that the elder son did not dare kill a goat without his permission. The elder son did not insult his father, as did his brother, by claiming his inheritance before his father's death.

(3) The text tells us that the younger son spent his money "in dissolute living." Although that may be part of it, nothing was said about prostitutes or sexual license. It was the elder son, who in complaining to his father, brought this charge. He "has devoured your property with prostitutes" (30). Significantly, the image most of us have of the younger son's activities in spending his money is drawn mostly from what his older brother said about him.

(4) The "pods that the pigs were eating" were probably carob pods. Although the seed of the carob is used today as a substitute for chocolate, and its taste is pleasant, the meat of the carob has a foul smell. The food that the pigs were eating was disgusting; yet, he would gladly have eaten it.

(5) The words that the NRSV translates as "put his arms around him" literally mean "fell on his neck." This is a vigorous, emphatic, emotional embrace.

(6) A robe, a ring, and sandals were all signs of welcome. The price of a robe in ancient times, when there were no synthetic materials, was high. Remember the significance of Joseph's many-colored robe? It signified a special relationship between Joseph and his loving father. Remember that the soldiers cast lots over Jesus' robe. Presumably, the prodigal came home in tatters and barefoot. His father ordered that he be given a robe for his body, sandals for his feet, and a ring for his adornment.

(7) The fatted calf means literally the grain-fed calf. Then, as now, some animals were given special food to make their meat particularly tender. The fatted calf would be one that had been set aside for a special occasion, and was being fed food that would make its meat more tender and tasty. This contrasts with the "young goat" that the elder son complained he never had.

(8) The elder son, although faithfully obedient to his father, did not show himself to be particularly close to him. He complained that he had worked "like a slave" rather than like a son. When he spoke of having a party, it was for a celebration "with my friends," in which the father apparently would have no place.

11

Luke 16:1–15

LEARNING FROM A SCOUNDREL

LEARNING MENU

Keeping in mind the ways in which your class members learn best as well as their needs and interests, choose at least one learning segment from each of the three Dimensions.

Dimension 1: What Does the Bible Say?

(A) Read the text.

● Invite a class member to read Luke 16:1-15 aloud.

(B) Answer the questions in the study book.

● Preferably, class members will have read the chapter and have answered the questions in Dimension 1 before the class session. If not, spend a brief amount of time discussing possible answers to the questions on page 86 of the study book. Answers to Dimension 1 questions are
   1. The disciples.

2. The main character in this parable is of questionable character, yet is praised for shrewdness.

3. The Pharisees ridiculed Jesus. Jesus reminded the Pharisees of their link to the manager in the parable.

(C) Recall stained-glass paintings.

● Read verses 1-8.
● Ask the class if they remember ever having studied this parable in Sunday school.
—Have you seen a painting or a stained-glass window about this parable?
—Which parables of Jesus have you seen depicted in art?
● List parables you have seen on chalkboard or newsprint. Some which you may have seen include the good Samaritan, the prodigal son, the rich man and Lazarus, and the sower. Make your list as long as possible. (In fact, you may wish to use this occasion simply as an opportunity for the class to rehearse how many of the parables of Jesus it can remember.)
● Ask:
—Is this parable more popular than any of those in that list? If so, why? If not, why not? (Obviously, the reason why this parable is not popular is that we prefer parables whose main characters are fairly decent. Here is a

parable about a scoundrel and a cheat, who still is set up as the main character of the parable!)

Optional Method: Make the same point by simply asking the class how they reacted to this parable as they read it in preparation for this session. Tell them to try to distinguish between what they think about it after having read the study book and what they thought about it before having read the study book. Encourage negative as well as positive responses. Then try to get people to express the reasons for those responses.
—What was it about the parable they didn't like?
● As a way to round out this discussion, you may wish to use another version of what is suggested in the previous option. Ask the class:
—If you had to choose three parables to be portrayed in large stained-glass windows in church, would you choose this one as one of the three? Why or why not?

Dimension 2:
What Does the Bible Mean?

This parable has an added factor that makes it difficult to interpret. It is not clear where the parable ends and its explanation begins. (The explanation itself may also be confusing.) You may find more information on the problem of where the parable ends in the Additional Bible Helps section on page 56. For the time being, center your attention on the first eight verses of the chapter and help the class analyze them.

(D) Tell the story of the dishonest manager.

● If your class normally participates easily and reads materials before coming to class (a practice you should encourage), it may suffice to ask one of them to tell the story of the dishonest steward. You may then give others opportunity to add anything that the first person missed or to clarify whatever was not clear.

As in most parables, the details are not important. What is important is the story itself. In order to communicate the point of the parable, it suffices to say that a steward who knew that he was about to be fired used his employer's wealth in order to feather his nest for the future. Still, you will want to give the class time to make certain that they all understand the story, so that you can then build on that common understanding.

(E) Read a modern version of the story.

● Read one or more of the following modern versions to the class.

A salesman had a fight with his boss. He knew that he could not continue working for the same company. So he took the company car and used his travel account to visit another city. There he had a job interview with the competition and offered to work for them and bring his list of clients with him. He even offered them some of the secrets he had learned from his current (and almost former) employer.

A woman learned that her husband was about to begin divorce proceedings. She had been a housewife all her life and was afraid that she would not be able to find employment at her age and with her lack of experience in the labor force. Knowing her husband would make every effort to get as much of the property as possible, she began withdrawing money from their joint account and stashing it away for the future, so that when she was actually divorced, she would have something on which to live.

● Ask the class these questions:
—Do you think these stories convey the point Jesus was making with the parable of the dishonest steward? If so, explain how. If not, why not?

(F) Explain the parable.

● Divide your study in two portions. Look first at verses 8-9. (At this point you may have to explain very briefly why it is so difficult to tell where the parable ends and the explanation begins.)
● Ignore for the time being the word *dishonest*. Ask:
—What do you understand by the words "make friends for yourselves by means of wealth so that when it is gone, they may welcome you into the eternal homes?" (In this context, *they* refers to the "friends" that one has made by means of wealth.)
—Is this what the steward did?
—Is this what the salesman did?
—Is this what the housewife did?

(G) Discuss the phrase "dishonest wealth."

● If you have ample time, and you feel that the class is ready for such a discussion, you may lead a discussion on the meaning of the phrase "dishonest wealth." For that discussion, you will need to note the points made in the Additional Bible Helps on page 57.
● Read aloud verses 10-13.
   These verses are somewhat complicated in their structure and are not necessary to understand the point of the parable. Therefore, you have two options:
—Simply ignore them and move on to the Pharisees and their reaction.

—If you have sufficient time, try to clarify their meaning.
- To do this, note that this passage consists of four verses and that each verse contrasts two things, one passing and one permanent.
- Write the following chart on the chalkboard or newsprint as someone reads the passage:

	passing	**permanent**
verse 10	very little	much
verse 11	dishonest wealth	true riches
verse 12	what belongs to another	what is your own
verse 13	master mammon	master God

- Share the following information with your class members:

> When you read these verses in this way, it is clear that, although some details might be confusing, the general drift is the same as that of the parable. We all have now at our disposal, in the world of unrighteousness, what may be termed "very little," or "unrighteous wealth," or "what belongs to another" (in other words, what "you can't take with you"). We can use all of this as if it were ultimate. This is to serve mammon as god. It is also foolish, since, like the steward, we should know that we are fired from the present order. But we can also use it in such a way that we will receive "much," or "the true riches," or "what is our own." In order to do this, we have to remember that our master is not mammon, but God. In other words, we have to use all we have in the service of God, and not in the service of the present god of wealth.

- Read aloud verses 14-15, which tell us of the reaction of the Pharisees.

(H) Consider the Pharisee's reaction.

- Ask the class:
—Is there any connection between the Pharisees being "lovers of money" and their reaction to what Jesus had just said?

(I) Imagine our reaction.

- Invite class members to imagine the reaction of our congregation if next Sunday the preacher used as an illustration one of the two stories told in exercise (E), the salesman or the housewife.
—Do you think the illustration will be well received? Why?
—Would your reaction be similar to that of the Pharisees? Would it be different? How?

(J) Place the parable in a figurative stained-glass window.

- If time allows, end the class by going back to the possibility of placing this parable on a stained-glass window.
- Ask the following question:
—Suppose that you are an artist and are told to design a window with this parable in it. How would you do it?

Dimension 3:
What Does the Bible Mean to Us?

(K) Explore alternatives.

The study book pointed out that the steward had two alternatives other than the one he chose. His first alternative was to decide that, since this was his employer's wealth and he had been given notice, he might as well live it up, using that wealth as long as he had authority over it. The second alternative was to tell himself that, since his employer would have nothing to do with him and could not guarantee his continuing employment, he would simply ignore his employer's wealth and act as if this situation did not exist.
- Ask the class:
—Do we see people today taking the first of these alternatives? (Most of our society is organized around this alternative. People do not want to be reminded of their "firing." In some cases, it seems that people believe that they will be immortalized through possessions. Make certain that the discussion does not deal only with "the rich and famous," but also with us.)
—To what extent is this a temptation for us?
- Explore the second alternative. This approach is often the religious or the philosophical one. Indeed, many religions argue that, since the goods of this world are all passing, the truly religious person will simply ignore them. Ask the class:
—Is this what Jesus was saying in this parable?
—Have you ever heard this attitude being taught in church?
—Are you ever tempted by this view?

(L) Consider the substance of our stewardship.

The parable talks about the use of wealth, but it can also be applied to all the other "goods" that we have in this life. Stewardship is not only of money, but also of time, abilities, and all other phases of life.
- Ask the class to make a list on chalkboard or newsprint of such items that should be the substance of our stewardship.

- Divide the class in groups of three to five members.
- Assign one item to each group. Ask each small group to discuss what the parable of the dishonest steward would mean as applied to that particular item.
—For instance, what would it mean if applied to the use of our time? (Obviously, we are given a limited supply of time in this life. We can waste it, since it is not really ours to keep. Or we can use it as people preparing for and announcing the reign of God. If we choose this last alternative, what sorts of things can we imagine doing with our time?)
- After allowing some time for discussion, bring the class back together and allow each group to report on its discussion.

(M) Affirm the idea of "You can't take it with you!"

- Write on the chalkboard or newprint in large letters: YOU CAN'T TAKE IT WITH YOU!!!
- Since this is a fairly generally accepted piece of common wisdom, the class will probably think that this is the point you are making. However, ask class members to look again at the parable. Consider:
—Did the steward find a way to "take it with him" after his firing became effective?
- Look at the two modern stories told in activity (E).
—Did the salesman find a way to "take it with him"?
—Did the homemaker find a way to "take it with her"?
- Clearly, what the parable says is that it is possible to "take it with you." Ask the class:
—What can we do to "take it with us"?

(N) Play a game.

- You must prepare for this option before class.
- Provide a number of 3-by-5 index cards. You will need to have enough cards to provide one card per participant.
- Divide the index cards into three stacks. Turn one stack into "play money" by writing different amounts on them (some could say $1,000; others could say $10,000; perhaps even one could say $1,000,000.) Turn the other stack into "play time" by writing on the individual cards a different number of hours a week (3 hours a week, 6 hours a week). Finally, turn the last stack into "play talents" by writing in each a different gift that people may have ("singing," "working with your hands," "teaching," and so forth). Shuffle all the cards together and bring them to class.
- To begin the game, invite each person to draw a card. The drawn card must be invested, according to the principles we have been discussing. In other words, it is something they must invest in view of their impending "firing" from this life and their hope for the reign of God.

- Participants may mingle and ask other's advice as to how to "invest" what they have been given. Allow a few minutes for this activity.
- Bring the group together and ask several individuals to say what they have decided to do with their "play money," "play time," or "play talents."
- Ask participants to think in silence:
—Are the principles which undergirded their decisions in the game the same principles by which they invest their actual money, time, and talents?
—If not, how could they change their lives?
- Encourage participants who wish to do so to share their thoughts.

(O) Examine quotations.

At the end of the teacher's materials for lesson 8, page 42, there was a list of quotations having to do with money and its use. If you did not use those quotes then, you may wish to look at them again, and see if there are any that might be worth discussing in connection with the parable we are studying today.

If you decide to use one of these quotes, you may wish to find out more about the person who said it. You may do so by looking up the person's name in a good dictionary of church history or in an encyclopedia.
- Read the quote aloud.
- Ask the class the following questions:
—Does the quotation express the same principles as the parable? Does it differ from the parable?
- After discussing a particular quotation, ask:
—How may the same principles be applied in other fields of stewardship such as the use of time or abilities?

Additional Bible Helps

Where Does a Parable End?

As has been mentioned above, one of the difficulties with the parable of the dishonest steward, besides the very fact that a dishonest person is used as an example, is the difficulty in determining exactly where the parable ends and its explanation begins.

In the ancient Greek manuscripts of the New Testament, there are no quotation marks. Therefore, when Luke says in verse 1 that "Jesus said to his disciples," we know that this is the beginning of a quote. But where does the quote end? In most cases, one can tell by the sense of the words. Here, the ambiguity of verse 8 makes that impossible.

In verse 8 we are told that "the master" commended the dishonest manager because he had acted shrewdly. The problem is that the word "master" (*kyrios*) is also a title that Luke often employed to refer to Jesus. Is this master Jesus? or is he the master of the dishonest steward? If the former, the parable has ended, and Jesus' commentary begins here. If the latter, the parable continues until verse 9, where Jesus says "and I tell you."

The NRSV decides the matter by translating "the master" as "his master"—that is, the steward's master. In this case, the parable continues until verse 9. The King James Version decides the matter in the opposite direction by translating "the lord," which clearly implies that this is Jesus now speaking. The Revised Standard Version reflects the ambiguity of the Greek text by saying "the master."

In truth, it is impossible to decide the matter simply on grammatical and linguistic grounds. In the foregoing, we have generally assumed that the parable ends in verse 7 and that from the beginning of verse 8 it is Jesus who is speaking. The reason for this is that the comments of "the master" in the second half of verse 8 are easier to understand as words of Jesus than as words of the fictitious "master" of the parable.

This does not greatly affect the interpretation of the text. The point of the parable is clearly the same no matter where it ends, or who "the master" in verse 8 is. If we have taken the time to explain it, it is because often in a class studying this parable, the question is raised, and you, as a teacher, will want to have the information necessary to answer it.

Dishonesty Merits Special Consideration

The term *dishonest* also merits special consideration. It appears five times in this passage in the NRSV Bible. In verse 8, the steward is called dishonest. In verses 9 and 11, it is a matter of "dishonest wealth." Finally, the same word appears twice in verse 10: "who is dishonest in a very little is dishonest also in much."

The phrase "dishonest wealth" (or, in the Revised Standard Version, "unrighteous mammon") has led to many debates and misunderstandings. At one extreme, there are those who say that this interpretation implies that the rich man had obtained his wealth dishonestly, and that therefore the steward was not really taking what belonged to his master. He was simply returning it to its rightful owners. This is a rather far-fetched interpretation, whose sole purpose is to exonerate the steward for his own dishonesty. At the other extreme, there are those who claim that this

means that all wealth is dishonest, inasmuch as it is taken from the poor. Many in the ancient church understood it to be so. Although there may be other grounds for such an attitude, this text does not really support that interpretation.

What the Greek text literally says is "the steward of unrighteousness," and "the mammon of unrighteousness." Since such phrases often function as adjectives, the NRSV translates them as "the unrighteous steward," and "unrighteous wealth."

If we look at verse 8, however, where Jesus is speaking of "the children of this age," it seems simpler to understand the phrase more literally. "This age" is an age of unrighteousness. Therefore, the steward of this age, who manages things of this age, is a "steward of unrighteousness." The wealth of this age is "wealth of unrighteousness," not because it has been fraudulently obtained, but because it is wealth of this age of unrighteousness.

Read the text again with this understanding in mind, and see if it does not make better sense than before.

The Parable of the Rich Man and Lazarus

Although we shall not study that parable in detail, you may wish to look ahead in your Bible to the parable of the rich man and Lazarus (Luke 16:19-31). Note that this parable was presented as part of Jesus' response to the Pharisees after they began criticizing what he had said regarding the dishonest steward and the proper management of the goods of the present age.

When you read it in this light, that parable may be seen as a further commentary or illustration of the parable of the unjust steward. In this case, it is the rich man who mismanaged what he had been given in this age. He did not "make friends" for himself by means of "the wealth of unrighteousness," which he possessed in this unrighteous age. Because he was not a good steward, he was punished in Hades. He was not received "into the eternal homes."

The end of that parable is a warning. It is addressed directly to the Pharisees, but also to any who have the power to manage wealth or other goods in this age of unrighteousness, and do it according to its unrighteous principles, rather than being guided by the righteousness that is to come.

12

Luke
23:26-49

$\mathcal{T}$HE CRUCIFIXION

LEARNING MENU

Keeping in mind the ways in which your class members learn best as well as their needs and interests, choose at least one learning segment from each of the three Dimensions.

Dimension 1:
What Does the Bible Say?

(A) Answer questions in the study book.

As class members arrive, encourage them to discuss among themselves the answers they individually provided to the questions in Dimension 1, page 95, of the study book. Possible answers include the following:

1. The various witnesses or participants in the Crucifixion included Simon of Cyrene, the crowds (all nameless), two criminals (also crucified on that day), soldiers, the centurion, and the women followers from Galilee. The responses to the Crucifixion varied: mourners beat their breasts and wailed, soldiers cast lots for Jesus' clothing, some simply stood and watched, while others watched and scoffed. One criminal sought forgiveness; the other crimi-

nal derided Jesus for his failure to save himself (and the criminals). Some watched the scene from a distance; others were very near.

2. Luke included persons who were considered "outsiders" as important participants or witnesses to the Crucifixion. This is quite consistent with the rest of Luke's Gospel.

(B) Read the text.

Invite a class member to read aloud Luke 23:26-49.

(C) Enter into a devotional period.

● Given the subject of today's lesson, you may wish to begin the session with a brief devotional meditation on the meaning of the cross. To do so expand on what is said in the study book under the heading "What to Watch For," page 94. Follow your remarks by a period of silent prayer and meditation.

(D) Explore the differences between various Gospel accounts.

As a way of drawing attention to Luke's particular narrative of the Crucifixion, you may wish to have your class realize the differences between the various Gospel accounts of the same event. You may do this in one of two ways:

Option 1:

- Assign a team of four people to prepare a brief presentation on the subject.
- Meet with the team a few days before the class session and read the stories together. Have each of the four concentrate on one of the stories (found in Matthew 27:32-56, Mark 15:21-41, Luke 23:26-49, and John 19:16b-37).
- As the person in charge of Luke reads that account aloud in small sections, the others will read silently the parallel account in the Gospel assigned to them. The reader of the Luke version may stop every few verses so that all four may compare what they have read.
- Make a list of the things that Luke did not say, that others did say, and also of the things that Luke said and others did not.
- Present this list to the class. Note particular emphases of Luke, rather than take a lot of time comparing all four Gospels as part of the class period. In so doing, you will attempt to make Luke's story more clear to the class. The report must be brief and to the point. Otherwise, this could take all the time you have.

Option 2:

- Read aloud the story of the Crucifixion as it is told in Luke.
- Ask the people on your right to note anything they hear in this account that they do not often hear in stories of the Crucifixion or things that they do not usually notice.
- Ask the group on your left to make a note of things they have heard about the Crucifixion that they do not hear in Luke's story. (Ask them, for instance, to think of the "seven last words" that are often preached in churches on Good Friday, and see how many Luke does not include.)
- After your reading, allow one or two minutes for people to report their thoughts and findings. Again, remember that this is just a preliminary procedure to get the class into the text, and should not take too much time.

Dimension 2:
What Does the Bible Mean?

(E) Engage in research.

If your group is good at doing independent research, and you have the resources of a good library in your church or in your town, you may consider the following exercise. Again, you will need to plan ahead so that class members can accomplish their research task.

- Assign different individuals to find out as much as they can about each of the following:

—Simon of Cyrene. This they can look up in a Bible dictionary.

—Women in Jewish tradition, especially when it came to fertility and barrenness. Most modern dictionaries of the Bible have articles on this topic. If not, look up the word *barren* in a concordance to discover the general attitudes toward a childless woman in the Old Testament (and also in the New Testament in the story of Elizabeth).

—The "leaders of the people." The person assigned this task may review the Gospel of Luke to learn about the attitudes of the religious leaders toward Jesus. In particular, examine the chapters after Jesus entered Jerusalem. (If the person assigned this task so wishes, it is possible to follow the same thread through the first seven chapters of Acts.)

—The Roman soldiers. How was the Roman army organized? From where did the recruits for the legions come? How long was their term of service? How would they be seen by good Jews in Jerusalem? To research this point, a book on the history of the Roman Empire would suffice. If not, some encyclopedias have good articles under the headings of "legion" and "legionnaire."

—The criminals. There is an excellent chapter (chapter 2) in *Bandits, Prophets, and Messiahs*, by Richard A. Horsley and John S. Hanson (Harper & Row, 1985). It is important to remember that bandits at this time were very often people from the lower classes who could not bear the burdens of taxes and debts, and therefore took to the wilderness. Thus, they were not entirely unpopular among the masses (see the references to Barabbas in the Gospels).

—The centurion. The person doing this research may collaborate with the person reporting on the soldiers.

—The women from Galilee. Read Luke 8:2-3, where some of these woman are mentioned by name. Then, with the aid of a concordance, see what else the Gospels say about them.

- During the week, follow up with these people by telephone or personal contact, to make sure they have done their research and offer them help if they need it.
- Assuming that researchers completed their task, read Luke's story aloud. Pause at appropriate times, to give each of the people who did the research an opportunity to say something about the particular characters mentioned in the story and what their presence in that place meant.

(F) Conduct optional research.

If you have not done activity (D), you may wish to use this method of researching the text.

- Read the text in sections, asking some of the following questions after each section:

Section 1, verses 26-31
—Do we know anything else about Simon of Cyrene?

(Look at the Additional Bible Helps, page 61.)

—What do you think was the attitude of the people following Jesus?

—What do you think is the meaning of the phrase "blessed are the barren" (29)?

—What do you think Jesus meant when he said, "For if they do this when the wood is green, what will happen when it is dry?"(31)

Section 2, verses 32-38

—Does anyone know the origin of the words *Calvary* and *Golgotha*? (They come from the Latin and Aramaic words for "skull.")

—Was crucifixion a common way of execution at the time? Who practiced it? (It was a fairly common way that the Romans employed in executing various criminals, particularly rebels.)

—Some Bibles have a note on part of verse 34, indicating that "other ancient authorities" do not have this sentence. Do you know what this means? (The various manuscripts that we have of the Gospel of Luke are not all identical. Some do not include this saying of Jesus.)

—Look at the word *but* in verse 35. Did Luke contrast "the people" with "the leaders?" If so, what do you think was the significance of this contrast?

—The inscription over Jesus was "This is the King of the Jews." Did that sign tell the truth? Why do you think this sign was put there?

Section 3, verses 39-43

—What do you think was the difference between the two criminals?

—The criminal asked Jesus to remember him. When did he want Jesus to remember him? Jesus answered with a promise to be fulfilled. When?

Section 4, verses 44-49

—At what time was Jesus crucified? (Some Bibles say "the sixth hour," and some say "noon." It is the same time.) At what time did his trial begin? (See Luke 22:66.) At what time did he die?

—What was the significance of the sun's failing and the curtain of the Temple being torn in two? (See the Additional Bible Helps, page 62.)

—What do you think is the significance of the centurion's statement? (Jesus was unjustly condemned. In Acts, Luke will follow a parallel theme, arguing that Christians were unjustly condemned. If your class would profit from it, you may point out that according to Matthew and Mark, what the centurion said was that Jesus was the Son of God.)

—What was the attitude of the crowds? Could these be the same crowds that shouted, "Crucify him!"? Could they be the same crowds that greeted him when he entered Jerusalem?

—Who do you think are the "acquaintances" to whom Luke referred here? (Luke did not tell. It is interesting, however that Joseph of Arimathea, whom Luke mentioned for the first time in verse 50, would have been just such an "acquaintance.")

—Who were "the women who had followed him from Galilee?" (See Luke 8:1-3.)

Dimension 3:
What Does the Bible Mean to Us?

(G) Draw parallels between Christmas and the Crucifixion.

● In the study book a number of parallels are drawn between Christmas and the Crucifixion. You may look at some of these and have the class discuss whether or not they see any significance in them.

● First, discuss the parallel between the manger (among animals) and the cross (between thieves). Jesus was born outside the inn, and he was crucified outside the city. There was a place for him neither in the inn nor in the city.

● Ask the following questions:

—Does this tell us anything about who Jesus is and how the world received him?

—Does it tell us anything about who we are to be if we are to receive him?

—Does it tell us anything about how the world might react to those who serve him and proclaim his name?

● Second, there is a contrast between the glory of God shining on the shepherds in the middle of the night and the sun being darkened in the middle of the day.

● Ask:

—What do you think Luke was trying to portray in that contrast?

—Was the Crucifixion a time of gloom?

—If so, why do we say it happened on "Good Friday?"

—Among Protestants, it has become customary to have, instead of a crucifix, (which shows Jesus on the cross) an empty cross (which we say is also a sign of the Resurrection). Do you think that sometimes we move too quickly through the Crucifixion to the Resurrection, without paying enough attention to the drama and the pain of the cross?

—How would our faith and our lives be different if we (a) remember only the cross, and never think about the Resurrection? (b) remember only the Resurrection and never think about the cross? (c) remember the Resurrection but also remember that Jesus arrived at it only through the suffering of the cross?

● Finally, there is the parallel between the beginning (when a Galilean virgin received the news of Jesus' coming birth) and the end (when a group of Galilean women watched from afar as Jesus died).

- If you wish to discuss this parallel, you can discuss it from several angles:
—We often think that women played a minor role in the Bible. Yet Luke began and ended his story focusing on women. What can you remember of these and other women in the Gospel of Luke?
—What does Luke's account tell us about the role of women in the church today?
—In first century Judaism, women were marginalized and so were Galileans. Is there any significance to the importance Luke gave to the "Galilean women?"
—Is there any connection between the importance that Luke gave women and Luke's repeated concern for the poor, the sick, and the oppressed?
—If so, what does this mean for the manner in which we live as Christians today?
—Who today are marginalized, as Galileans and women were?
—What would it mean to preach "good news" to them?

(H) Consider a modern-day story.

If in presenting Dimension 2 (What Does the Bible Mean?) you followed activity (D), you will have class members who are fairly well acquainted with the background and attitudes of the various characters around the cross. Therefore, you may wish to relate this passage to our present life using these people's research and expertise as follows:

- Divide the class into four groups. Each group should consider one of the following persons or groups:
—Simon of Cyrene;
—the women (both at the beginning of the passage and at the end);
—the leaders of the people;
—the soldiers and the centurion.
- Assign the person(s) who did the corresponding research to each of the groups.
- Give each group a piece of paper with the following story:

It was a very nice neighborhood in the city of Metropolis. At least, everyone thought so until the man Joshua arrived. He seemed nice. Most people liked him. He even did them some favors, and for that they were grateful. Then, one day he began bringing homeless people into his nice home. When he brought the first one, some people said that was very nice of him. Others did not like it. By the time there were ten homeless people in Joshua's house, community leaders decided that something ought to be done about it. They took Joshua to court and sued him. Joshua never had a chance. People were afraid of what he was doing. Eventually, he lost his house.

- Ask each group to add something to the story, giving a role to someone like the one Bible character(s) they have been assigned. (For instance, the "soldiers" might decide to add police officers to the story, and to say something about their role in it. Or Simon of Cyrene might be a bystander who somehow gets involved.) Give each group a few minutes to brainstorm about how they would make that addition to the story.
- Bring the class back together and have groups report their discussion.
- Challenge each member of the class to think about their various roles in today's church and society, and whether this discussion tells them anything about their own Christian life and obedience.

(I) Discover imagery of a poem.

Luke gave no explanation nor reason for the Crucifixion. While he told us repeatedly that Jesus announced his own death, he did not attempt to give a theological explanation of the significance of the Crucifixion. We cannot, however, read this story without immediately facing the question of its significance for us.

American poet Edward Taylor did face this question in the poem quoted in the study book, page 98.

- Once again, invite a class member to read the poem aloud while the rest of the class follows the reading in their own books. (Since the language is rather archaic, this may be necessary so that all can understand the words.) Do the same with the sonnet by Lope de Vega, page 96.
- Select some of the images in those poems.
—Consider first Taylor's image: "Didst make thyselfe Deaths marke shot at for mee?" What does that line mean? Do we feel that this describes what Jesus does for us in the cross? Why? Why not? Would you put it another way?
—Look at the last line of Lope's sonnet: "With feet nailed to the cross, thou art waiting still for me." What does that line mean? Do you feel that this line describes what Jesus does for us in the cross? Why? Why not? Would you put it another way?

Additional Bible Helps

Simon of Cyrene

Cyrene was in North Africa and had a fairly large Jewish population. Jews from Cyrene were mentioned repeatedly by Luke in Acts. They were among those present at Pentecost (2:10); among those who challenged Stephen (6:9); as Christians who took the lead in preaching in Antioch (11:20); and as leaders of the church in Antioch (13:1).

In a passage parallel to the one we are studying, Mark 15:21 said that Simon of Cyrene was "the father of

Alexander and Rufus." Apparently, these names were known in the community for which Mark wrote, but not to Luke's audience. (A "Rufus" was mentioned in Romans 16:13, but there is no way of knowing if this was the same as Simon's son.)

Finally, there is another intriguing possibility. In Acts 13:1, Luke mentioned among the "prophets and teachers" of the church in Antioch "Simeon who was called Niger" and "Lucius of Cyrene." Simon's surname means "black." Could it be that "Simon of Cyrene" was a dark-skinned man from that area, and that Lucius was a compatriot of his? The conjecture has often been made, but there is no way to prove or disprove it.

Consider the Cross

The cross that Simon carried was in all probability very different from what we usually see in pictures or movies. The common form of the cross as we now see it is called the Latin cross and is not the form of the crosses on which crucifixions usually took place. The cross used for crucifixion is usually called the *Tau* cross (from the name of the Greek letter *Tau*, *T*). It is shaped like a *T*, rather than like a Latin cross. Usually the vertical member of the cross was already implanted on the ground. The person to be executed was then fixed (either tied or nailed) to the horizontal beam, which was then lifted with the person on it and fixed on top to form the cross. Sometimes, since that horizontal member was the crosspiece, it was called the cross. Therefore, in a crucifixion where the condemned was forced to carry the cross, this probably meant the horizontal beam from which he was to hang.

Jesus Called Sinners to Repentence

The word that Luke used for those who were crucified with Jesus, and which the NRSV translates as "crimi-nals," literally means "evil-doers." Here Luke used a different word than Mark and Matthew, who used a term that can be understood to refer to a revolutionary bandit or rebel. Luke apparently wished to make it clear that the men crucified with Jesus, of whom one turned to him for help, were no popular revolutionary heroes, but two common criminals. In a way, this is the culmination of a theme that we have seen throughout the Gospel of Luke: Jesus came to call sinners to repentance. That is why he ate with publicans and sinners. That is why, at the very last moment, he forgave, promising life to a convicted common criminal.

What About the Temple Curtain?

The reference to the curtain of the Temple is not altogether clear. There were thirteen different curtains in the Temple. Of these, the most likely candidate for Luke's reference was the one separating the holy of holies from the rest of the Temple. This was the most important of all the Temple curtains, and therefore Luke's reference to "the curtain" should probably be taken to refer to it.

That, however, still leaves open the question of the meaning of the reference itself. The most common interpretation is that, because of Jesus' death, sacrifices would no longer be required, and the holy of holies would now be open. This interpretation reflects the teachings of Hebrews 9:11-22, where Jesus "entered once for all the Holy Place, not with the blood of goats and calves, but with his own blood, thus obtaining eternal redemption."

Another interpretation, however, understands the tearing of the curtain as the breaking down of the wall of separation between Jew and Gentile. Finally, a third interpretation sees this event as a sign of the coming destruction of Jerusalem, and that destruction as punishment for the rejection and the death of Jesus.

13

**Luke
24:13-35**

THE WALK TO EMMAUS

LEARNING MENU

Keeping in mind the ways in which your class members learn best as well as their needs and interests, choose at least one learning segment from each of the three Dimensions.

Dimension 1:
What Does the Bible Say?

Under this dimension, we will explore common threads or themes appearing in Luke's Gospel. The purpose is to use this lesson as a review of all that we have studied during these three months—a review, not in the sense of repeating all of it, but rather in the sense of tying it all together.

(A) Read the passage.

● Read aloud the story of the walk to Emmaus as told in Luke 24:13-35.

(B) Study the map.

● Using a good Bible map, find the probable location of Emmaus (about 7 miles northwest of Jerusalem) and the probable route taken by the disciples.

(C) Identify four themes of Luke.

● Refer to Dimension 1, page 103, of the study book and note the four themes or interests of Luke—wonders, teaching, women, and meals.
● Record each of the four themes on chalkboard or newsprint, so that each word heads a column of a four-column chart. As class members discuss the four themes, note significant comments on the chart, under the appropriate column.
● Regarding each theme, ask these questions:
—Where do we see this in the text we are studying?
—Does this remind us of anything we have already studied in the Gospel of Luke? (In order to facilitate this discussion, leaders should prepare by reviewing the twelve previously studied lessons, noting information regarding the four themes of wonders, teaching, women, and meals.)

(D) Study the text.

A common practice in many Sunday school classes is to read the text by going around the room, with each participant reading a verse, until the entire passage is read. This practice helps to get all students involved; but it has the great disadvantage of being difficult to follow a text read in this fashion. The option suggested here allows for similar general participation, but at the same time helps the entire class understand the text more fully.

● Since the class has already been together for some time, and you have given assignments before, you may be able to divide the text among the various participants the week before. If the class is large enough, assign one verse to a person. If not, assign two or three verses, as necessary.
● Each person is to study her or his assigned text as carefully as possible, thinking about comments they could make in class in order to clarify and explain the text. For instance, the person working on verse 13 could say something about "that same day" (same as what?) or about Emmaus (by looking it up in a Bible dictionary or a commentary). If that person reads more than one version of the Bible, it will become apparent that some versions say "seven miles," while others say "sixty stadia," and still others might say "a hundred and sixty stadia." (Why?) Similarly, the person working on verse 14 may ask, "What does Luke mean by 'these things that had happened'?"
● When the class convenes, the text will be read by these people, verse by verse, while the rest of the class follows the reading in their own Bibles. (This is important, so that all participants can follow the reports.) As each person reads his or her assigned text, that person makes brief comments, or offers clarifications. Make certain that they take no more than a minute average on each verse.
● After the entire passage has been read, open the class to a general discussion about the text itself, particularly about any aspects that may still be unclear.

(E) Meet the characters.

● As a class member reads aloud the text, list on chalkboard or newsprint all the principle characters in the story. Include both those present and those to whom others refer. This list will include such persons as "two of them," "Jesus," "Cleopas," "chief priests and leaders."
● At the end of the reading ask these questions:
—What do we know about each of these?
—What is their role in the story?

(F) Provide Additional Bible Study Helps.

● Drawing upon the Additional Bible Study section, pages 66-67, share additional information about the Bible passage with your class members.

(G) Draw parallels to the Christmas story.

● After reading the text, ask the class to think about the story of the shepherds watching over their flocks at night in the Christmas story. Ask:
—Can you see any parallels? (In both stories there is a movement from fear or perplexity to joy; in both stories that joy culminates in their seeing Jesus; in both stories they go out and tell.)
● Lead the class in a discussion:
—Do you think that some of these parallels are clues to what Luke is trying to tell us in his Gospel?

In the study book, we drew conclusions from this text in three different directions: (1) The meaning and significance of the resurrection of Jesus; (2) the importance of Scripture for the life of faith; and (3) the "breaking of the bread" as a means of recognizing and celebrating the presence of Jesus among us. As you choose from among the following options, consider which of these points would be most profitable for your group. It may be wise, rather than trying to make all three points, to center your attention on the theme of the Resurrection and the celebration of Easter. Then, if you have time, you may wish to pick up on either point two or three. (Note that, in a way, point three serves as a bridge into the Book of Acts. Therefore, if you plan to start studying that book soon, you may wish to take some time to deal with it.)

> **Point 1: The significance of the resurrection of Jesus**

(H) Make a statement.

Make the following statement, which is historically correct: "In the early church, the most important celebration was Easter. In fact, in the earliest time, every Sunday was considered a little Easter, and there was then the Great Easter in Holy Week. It was only later that the church began to celebrate the birth of Jesus with a special day. Even then, Easter was more important than Christmas. Today, it is obvious that Christmas has become a more important day than Easter."

● Ask:
—Why do you think this has happened?
—Do you think it is good? Why? Why not?

(I) Consider hymns.

● Read also the following lines, from some well-known hymns:

"Soar we now where Christ has led, Alleluia!
Following our exalted Head, Alleluia!
Made like him, like him we rise, Alleluia!
Ours the cross, the grave, the skies, Alleluia!"
("Christ the Lord Is Risen Today")

"The three sad days are quickly sped;
he rises glorious from the dead;
all glory to our risen head! Alleluia!"
("The Strife Is O'er, the Battle Done")

● Ask:
—What do you think these images mean?
—Do they help you understand the meaning of the resurrection of Jesus?
—Do these images give you a new perspective on what we mean when we say that we are "the body of Christ," and that he is "the head of the body"?

Point 2: The role of Scripture in the life of faith

(J) Read verses 25-27.

● Once again, read aloud verses 25-27.
● Point out that Jesus did not tell these disciples that they have not read the Bible enough. Nor did he say that they have not given the Bible sufficient authority. That was not their problem. Their problem seemed to be that they had read the Scriptures. They knew what they said, but did not understand. Since all the early disciples of Jesus were Jews, one may surmise that, like most Jews of their time, these two disciples knew the Scriptures rather well. They probably knew them better than most of us! Still, Jesus said that they were "foolish" and "slow of heart to believe." In other words, the problem was not in the amount of reading, but rather in the manner of it.
● Ask the class:
—As you read this story, what do you think was the difference between the manner these disciples were reading the Bible, and the manner in which Jesus was trying to get them to read it? (Note that verse 27 says that Jesus "interpreted to them the things about himself in all the scriptures." In other words, Jesus interpreted the Scriptures as referring to himself. He was teaching these two disciples to read the Scriptures in the same way, as referring to himself. If the heart of the message of Scrip-

ture is Jesus, all reading must somehow relate to him and to our obedience to him.)
● On the basis of the same verses 25-27, make the point that the most significant Bible reading takes place when, in our study of Scripture, we come to see Jesus himself and what he demands of us. When this awareness happens, we may have an experience similar to these two disciples, who felt their heart "burning" within themselves.
● Ask for testimonials of times when, in reading the Bible, members of the class have had the experience of an encounter with Christ, or a clearer vision of what obedience to him entails. Suggest that, since this is the last of our studies on the Gospel of Luke, some of these testimonials may refer to a biblical passage that we have studied during these thirteen sessions.

(K) Consider the value of other passages.

● Suggest one or two passages from the Hebrew Scriptures that you think Jesus could have quoted in his conversation with the two disciples on the road to Emmaus (for instance, Isaiah 53).
● Ask for other suggestions from class members. From this, you may easily move on to requesting testimonials such as those mentioned above, under activity (J).

Point 3: The "breaking of the bread" as a means of recognizing and celebrating the presence of Jesus among us

---

(L) Compare the meals of Emmaus and the upper room.

● Call attention to the sidebar in the study book, page 106, comparing the meal at Emmaus with the Lord's Supper at the upper room.
● Make the point that the parallels show that, in telling the story, Luke was clearly trying to tell us that the encounter at Emmaus was connected with the Last Supper. Jesus, who broke bread with the disciples at the Last Supper, was made known again to the disciples "in the breaking of the bread."
● Share the following information:
At Emmaus the mood was different from the Last Supper. In the upper room the impending betrayal and Crucifixion were hanging over the entire scene. Here, the breaking of the bread resulted in the joy of knowing that Jesus was alive! The next time Luke spoke of the "breaking of the bread" was early in the Book of Acts, when describing the life of the earliest Christian community. There, Luke says that "they devoted themselves to . . . the breaking of the bread" (Acts 2:42) and that "they

broke bread at home and ate their food with glad and generous hearts" (Acts 2:46).

- Point out that in those passages Communion is seen as a joyful occasion. It is the time when the risen Lord was made known to us, as earlier at Emmaus, "in the breaking of the bread." Tell the class that in the early church every Sunday was considered a "little Easter," because it was the day of the resurrection of the Lord, and that it was therefore a day of joy and celebration.
- Ask these questions:
—When we have Communion, is it a joyous or a somber occasion?
—In our minds, do we connect Communion primarily with Easter or with Good Friday?

(M) Compare Holy Communion rituals.

The following are three different invitations to the Lord's Table.

- Read each aloud or record them on newsprint or chalkboard so that the entire class can read them:
—All ye that do truly and earnestly repent of your sins and are in love and fellowship with your neighbors, and intend to live a new life, following the commandments of God and walking from henceforth in his holy ways, draw near with faith and take this holy sacrament to your comfort. (From *The Hymnal of the Evangelical United Brethren Church*, 1957; page 17)
—Christ our Lord invites to his table all who love him, who earnestly repent of their sin and seek to live in peace with one another. Therefore, let us confess our sin before God and one another. (From "A Service of Word and Table I," *The United Methodist Hymnal*, 1989; page 7)
—Friends, this is the joyful feast of the people of God! [They] will come from east and west, and from north and south, and sit at table in the kingdom of God. According to Luke, when our risen Lord was at table with his disciples, he took the bread, and blessed and broke it, and gave it to them. Then their eyes were opened and they recognized him. This is the Lord's table. Our Savior invites those who trust him to share the feast which he has prepared. (From *The Worship Book,* Westminster, 1970; page 34)
- Ask:
—Which of these is most somber? which most joyful?
—Which makes you think of Good Friday? which of Easter?
—Which reminds you most clearly of the meal at Emmaus?
—Which do you think would be most appropriate in the "breaking of the bread" that Luke describes in Acts 2:42 and 46?

(N) Look at hymns.

Instead of comparing rituals (or parts of rituals) for Holy Communion, look at hymns.

- Use the hymnbook most commonly used in your church, and look at the hymns that appear under the heading of "Holy Communion," "Eucharist," or "Lord's Supper."
- Ask:
—How many hymns seem more appropriate for Good Friday and how many for Easter? (You may quickly assign a different hymn to each participant in the class; then ask him or her to look for crucial words or phrases that set either a somber or a joyous mood. Invite each class member to report on their findings.

(O) Consider the regularity of Holy Communion in your congregation.

- Explain to the class that in the early church, and throughout most of the history of the church, the central act of Christian worship has been Communion, which most Christians have celebrated regularly every Sunday. John Wesley, for example, took Communion at least once a week.
- Ask:
—How often do we have Communion in our church?
—Do you think we should have it more often? Why, or why not?
- If someone expressed the opinion that it would be repetitious, ask the question:
—Why is that a problem for us—which it really is—and why is it not a problem for so many Christians in so many countries through so many centuries?

(P) Experience a service of Holy Communion.

Since you are now reaching the end of this study of Luke, you may wish to close this study with a celebration of Holy Communion.

- Arrange with the pastor to serve Holy Communion either at the regular worship service or as part of a worship service within the class period.
- If convenient, invite one or more members of the class to bake the bread together during the week.

Additional Bible Helps

More About the Emmaus Event
Regarding verse 13, there are several elements that may be clarified. Within the teaching plan itself, reference has been made to the phrase "on that same day." The phrase "two of them" may have been two men, as we usually imagine, or a man and a woman. The phrase here is in the

plural masculine; but Greek uses the plural masculine to refer, not only to groups of men, but also to mixed groups of men and women. The "seven miles" are an approximate equivalent of the "sixty stadia" to which most manuscripts refer, although there are other manuscripts that speak of 160 stadia (closer to twenty miles). The village of Emmaus is not known apart from this story. It must have been a small hamlet in the outskirts of Jerusalem. In that case, by now it must have been swallowed up by the city in its growth.

The phrase in verse 28, "he walked ahead as if he were going on," may give the impression that Jesus tried to deceive his two companions. That, however, is not its meaning, when we take into account the customs of the time. It was impolite for a traveler to presume on other people's hospitality. It was equally impolite to refuse hospitality to a stranger who had no place to stay. Thus, the normal ritual was for the stranger to continue as if not expecting hospitality, and for the prospective hosts then to invite the stranger. (In Hispanic culture there is a similar ritual. If one is a guest at another's table, and is offered something to eat, one is expected to refuse. The host then insists once more. It is at that time that the guest is free to either accept or refuse the invitation. The first refusal, although not quite expressing the guest's desire, is not considered dishonest. It is simply a social convention.)

An Act of Contrition or Celebration?
In the early church, Communion was more a celebration that an act of contrition. People related the act of Holy Communion with Easter, rather than with Good Friday. This was the understanding for the first five or six centuries of the history of the church (and is still the case in the Eastern churches, such as the Greek and the Russian Orthodox). What happened? In the West, after the fall of the Roman Empire, there ensued a period of chaos in which death and suffering became very real, daily occurrences. In that sort of situation, religion turned more

somber, and Holy Communion took on more of the characteristics of a Good Friday than an Easter service. It is in recent years that most major denominations have begun to rediscover the original joyous mood of Holy Communion—particularly its connection with Easter. For that reason, if you compare the manner in which Holy Communion was celebrated in most major denominations fifty years ago, and the way it is celebrated now, you will see that there has been a clear movement away from a Good Friday mood and towards an Easter mood. (This trend is especially seen in the hymns that various hymnals include under the heading of "Eucharist," "Holy Communion," or "Lord's Supper." That is why the teaching plan for this session suggested that you might wish to look at those hymns with your class and discuss their mood.)

We often forget another dimension of Holy Communion as celebrated by the early church, and which has not even been mentioned in our lesson. This is its pointing towards the coming reign of God. When early Christians celebrated Holy Communion, they were not only remembering the Last Supper and celebrating the resurrection of Jesus, but also looking forward to the day of the great heavenly banquet (an image that appears repeatedly in the Bible, particularly in the Book of Revelation). That is why at Holy Communion Christians prayed "Maranatha"—"Come, Lord"—or "Come, Lord Jesus." The oldest Holy Communion prayer that we have points precisely to that end time of joy and celebration. That prayer, which comes from an ancient document called "The Teaching of the Twelve Apostles," has been translated into a hymn:

As grain, once scattered on the hillsides,
Was in this broken bread made one,
So from all lands thy Church be gathered
Into the kingdom of thy Son.
(From *The Book of Hymns*, No. 307; The United Methodist Publishing House, 1964. Used by permission of the Church Pension Fund.)

CALLED TO TEACH IN THE HOUSEHOLD OF GOD

by Linda J. Vogel

> On their return the apostles told Jesus all they had done. He took them with him and withdrew privately to a city called Bethsaida. When the crowds found out about it, they followed him; and he welcomed them, and spoke to them about the kingdom of God, and healed those who needed to be cured.
>
> The day was drawing to a close, and the twelve came to him and said, "Send the crowd away, so that they may go into the surrounding villages and countryside, to lodge and get provisions; for we are here in a deserted place." But he said to them, "You give them something to eat." They said, "We have no more than five loaves and two fish—unless we are to go and buy food for all these people." For there were about five thousand men. And he said to his disciples, "Make them sit down in groups of about fifty each." They did so and made them all sit down. And taking the five loaves and the two fish, he looked up to heaven, and blessed and broke them, and gave them to the disciples to set before the crowd. And all ate and were filled. What was left over was gathered up, twelve baskets of broken pieces.
>
> (Luke 9:10-17)

Whenever we share in a baptism in our congregations, we hear words such as these from the United Methodist prayer of thanksgiving over the water: "In the fullness of time you sent Jesus, nurtured in the water of a womb. He was baptized by John and anointed by your Spirit. He called his disciples to share in the baptism of his death and resurrection and to make disciples of all nations" (From the "Baptismal Covenant I," *The United Methodist Hymnal*; 1989; page 36). As we welcome the newly baptized into the household of

God, we are urged to remember our baptism and be thankful.

As disciples of Jesus Christ and members of Christ's family, the church, we are all called to use our gifts in ways that share with others the good news of God's love for all persons and nations. Some of us are asked by our church family to be teachers. It is a real privilege and a great responsibility to be called to teach. It is one way that we can live out the vows of our baptism.

Perhaps you are thinking, "Who, me?" or "Why me?" or "If I could, I would, but . . . ." You are in good company! Moses argued with God about his call. He didn't have a gift with words and, besides that, he was wanted for murder in Egypt. Surely God could see that this call was asking the impossible! Jeremiah was just a young boy and was sure that he could not do what he was being asked to do. Mary had difficulty comprehending the meaning of the gift she was to receive as well. Time and time again, the disciples failed to understand. They sometimes lacked faith. They pled with Jesus to see things their way even when it was not God's way.

So, it seems, we are in good company if we feel inadequate for the task that is ours. But we can find comfort in realizing that God used all of these imperfect ones to share the good news of God's faithfulness and love. God can and will use you and me as teachers called to "walk the walk *and* talk the talk" with others as we journey in faith.

Teaching as Jesus Taught

The biblical account of Jesus feeding the five thousand is the only miracle story found in all four Gospels (Matthew 14:13-21; Mark 6:30-44; Luke 9:10-17; John 6:1-15). In this significant event, Jesus offers us a model for what it means to teach and learn with those who seek to know Jesus.

This story is about meeting people where they are and addressing the real life needs that they have. The needs of the crowd conflicted with the desperate need that Jesus and the disciples had to rest. John the Baptist had been beheaded. They were grieving and wondering about the meaning of his death. Yet Jesus put aside his plans and attended to the needs of the crowd.

It is about letting go of our assumptions and questions. The disciples wanted to send the people away. They reminded Jesus that it would cost more than a farm worker could earn in two hundred days to feed all these people. Their view of the world and their own situation could not accommodate the needs of the multitude. Either they had to send the people away or they had to expand their horizon and gain a new perspective on the situation.

It is about reframing questions and focusing on new ways of thinking about the resources at hand. "How much bread do you have? Go and see!" introduces a totally new way of thinking and acting. Asking questions that cause persons to consider an issue in a new way may be more important than giving answers.

The accounts of this event remind us that Jesus did not allow people to remain a part of the multitude. Rather, he urged his disciples to create a safe and hospitable space by organizing a crowd of tired and hungry people into groups of fifty and one hundred and having them sit down on the green grass. Being called to teach is about welcoming learners into an inviting space where they feel free to open themselves to growing and learning with others.

Jesus drew on familiar stories and rituals of faith as he took food that was given to be shared, looked up to heaven, gave thanks, and broke the bread. This ritual act must have rekindled memories in these pilgrims who had turned aside to see Jesus on their way to Jerusalem to celebrate the Passover. They must have recalled that first Passover meal which marked the beginning of God's deliverance of the chosen people as Moses led them out of slavery toward the Promised Land; manna in the wilderness; Passover meals celebrated every year with their families as they remembered the promises of God.

After the Resurrection, those two disciples who walked from Jerusalem to Emmaus must have remembered the feeding of the multitude when they recognized Jesus in the breaking of the bread. And the disciples who shared an early morning breakfast of fish on the shore of Galilee with the risen Jesus must have recalled how they had fed those hungry pilgrims.

Recalling and telling the stories of faith is one of the ways teachers are called to share. Stories of faith help us make connections—connections which link our past, present, and future; connections between who God is and who God calls us to be.

When all the men, women, and children had eaten and were full, Jesus instructed the disciples to gather up the leftovers. They collected twelve baskets full of food. Jesus shows us that it is necessary to assess what we have done and what we have left that may help us as we move into the future. Teaching, learning, serving, and evaluating are all a part of the whole.

Claiming Our Call to Teach

As persons called to teach, we may find courage when we recognize that the disciples—when Jesus empowered to feed the multitude—did not understand all they needed to understand. They asked the wrong questions; they seemed to put their own needs ahead of the needs of the crowd. They could not conceive of any way that Jesus could or reason that Jesus should feed all those folks! In spite of their lack of understanding and vision, they became servant-teachers. We too can teach and serve; not knowing enough does not disqualify us either.

Calls to teach come in many ways. Sometimes we have a sense deep within us that this is what God would have us do. Sometimes it comes in the form of an invitation from a member of the education committee or a pastor. They may tell you that they have prayed and believe that you have the gifts that are needed to teach a particular class. At other times we see a need and want to meet it. *Call* has been aptly described as the intersection where our gifts and the world's needs meet.

However we came to this place, it is good to name and claim our role as a teacher in the household of God. We can step out in faith to meet people where they are and to invite them to address the real life issues and situations in which they find themselves. As teachers we are called to create a safe and hospitable space where persons can be open and honest about who they are and about the doubts and questions that they have. This requires us to let go of many of our assumptions in order to listen with empathy and to see the world through the learners' eyes. It calls us to reframe our questions and focus on new ways of thinking and acting. Being a teacher requires us to learn to share the stories of faith and to join others in celebrating the church's rituals. As we listen to the stories and questions of the learners, we may be able to help them make connections between their stories and the Faith Story and between past, present and future. As teachers it is our responsibility to help learners assess where they are and what resources they have and will need as they continue to journey in faith.

We can be empowered by knowing who we are and claiming our call as a teacher in the household of God. May we claim our call to teach as we accept the task proclaimed in song, "We call each new disciple to follow thee, O Lord, redeeming soul and body by water and the Word." ("Go, Make of All Disciples," From *The Book of Hymns*, Abingdon Press, 1964.)

From Teacher in the Church Today, *May 1992; pages 3-5. Copyright © 1992 by Cokesbury.*

HOW THE BIBLE CAME TO BE

by Cheryl Reames

We think of the Bible as one book. Yet, in a sense it is many books. The Bible contains many kinds of writings, including historical narratives, laws, wise sayings, prophetic utterances, poetry, liturgies, gospels, letters, sermons, and apocalypses.

Many different people wrote the different books of the Bible over many periods of time and history. Usually, the books first circulated independently. Gradually, people gathered the books into small collections. Then they made collections of the collections, until finally the Bible came together in the form we know today. Yet, even though the Bible is a collection of many books written and gathered together over more than a thousand years, it has one theme: God's actions to redeem God's chosen, obedient people.

The Canon

Canon comes from a word that meant *reed*. A reed was straight and could be used as a measuring rod. So, *canon* came to mean a standard by which other things are measured. When we apply the word *canon* to the Bible, we usually mean the official list or collection of Holy Scriptures.

The church did not apply the term *canon* to the Bible until a few centuries after the birth of Christ, when various events caused certain writings (in what we now call the canon) to become known as Scripture. Before books became officially accepted as Scripture, however, they were important in the life and worship of the people.

The Canon of the Old Testament
Oral Tradition

The first part of the Old Testament goes back to very ancient sources, about two thousand years before the birth of Christ. Before any of the Bible was written, there was a long period of oral transmission. During this time, the main outline of the Pentateuch (the first five books of the Old Testament) was taking shape. Especially were the stories told during Israel's great religious festivals.

We must recognize that Israel's transmission through oral tradition was very different from our idea of oral transmissions. Today we rely primarily on written material to preserve what is important. In Bible times, people relied primarily on oral narration to preserve what was important.

Oral tradition was vital during the whole period covered by the Old Testament. People learned by heart what was meaningful to them. They trained their memories to be very retentive. Oral tradition was not a haphazard recollection but a trained remembering.

The Law

Jewish tradition regards the books of Genesis, Exodus, Leviticus, Numbers, and Deuteronomy as the most authoritative of Jewish Scriptures. They are called the *Torah*, which means law or teaching. They are also called the *Pentateuch,* which means five scrolls.

In reading the Pentateuch, we recognize many inconsistencies, repetitions, and irregularities. Biblical scholars believe that this is because the Pentateuch is a composite of several sources blended together. The various differences reflect the faith of different historical periods. According to this theory, four main strands, traditions, or written sources exist. Scholars refer to these sources as J, E, D, and P.

We must not, however, think of these sources as following one another chronologically. The dates given below are approximate times when the material was written down. The sources of the material are much older. The various sources should be considered parallel traditions coming from ancient times. Each of the different traditions—J, E, P, and D—was developed and preserved in a particular circle of persons.

Scholars believe that the J source is the earliest, coming from about the tenth century B.C. They suggest that the E source comes from the Northern Kingdom about the eighth century B.C. The D source, which is best seen in the Book of Deuteronomy, comes from the Southern Kingdom around the seventh century B.C. The P source, representing priestly interests, comes from the time after the fall of the Southern Kingdom in 587 B.C.

First, J and E were blended together so closely that it is almost impossible now to separate them. The Deuteronomic (D) portion was inserted next. Then a priestly editor (P) took the block of JED material and enlarged it by inserting his tradition.

Somewhere between 427 and 397 B.C., Ezra read "the book of the law of Moses" to the people in a covenant ceremony (Nehemiah 8:1–10:39). There is some question about which book of the law Ezra read to the people. If it was the Pentateuch, this was the official establishment of the Pentateuch as the authority or canon for Jewish faith and practice.

The Prophets

The Jews after the Exile had other popular books, such as Joshua, Judges, Samuel, and Kings. They also recognized some books that contained prophetic oracles. But they did not yet consider these other books to be divinely revealed.

Public interest in these books, as well as their value to national pride and hope, resulted in their later acceptance into the canon. The writings that include the early and later prophets became a collection about the second century B.C. From about that time, they were regarded as Scripture. By the time of Jesus, it was standard to refer to Jewish Scripture as "the Law and the Prophets."

The Writings

Not until about A.D. 90 did Jewish leaders begin to determine as canon the rest of the writings in the Hebrew Bible. About that time, a council of rabbis gathered at Jamnia to try to determine which of those writings should be authoritative for Jewish faith and life. This determination was completed by the third century A.D. Although we know which books the Jews accepted as authoritative, we do not know the exact standards by which they judged the books.

We do know several reasons that led to the canonization of Jewish Scriptures. The Jewish revolutionary movements against Rome were collapsing, so the Jewish leaders felt a need to ban apocalyptic literature that supported these movements. Christianity had arisen with a literature that the Jews considered heretical. The Septuagint or Greek Old Testament had become popular in the Christian church and began to be disfavored by the Jews.

The Apocrypha

What Christians call the Old Testament is not the same in Jewish, Eastern Orthodox and Roman Catholic, and Protestant Bibles. After the council of Jamnia and from the second century A.D., the Hebrew Bible has consisted of the thirty-nine books included in the Protestant Old Testament. However, in the Hebrew Bible they are grouped in such a

way that they number twenty-four. They are also in a different order. The Hebrew Bible groups the books as the Law (the Pentateuch), the Prophets, and the Writings.

Greek-speaking Jews of the Greco-Roman world and early Christians used a Greek translation of the Hebrew Bible called the Septuagint. Jewish scholars in Alexandria, Egypt made this translation sometime during the third and second centuries B.C. These Greek translators did not follow the three divisions that are now found in the Hebrew Bible. They arranged the books into topics: the Pentateuch, historical books, poetical books, and prophetical books.

The Septuagint contained the twenty-four books of the Hebrew Bible, but it also contained other books or portions of books. Most of these make up the Apocrypha. Roman Catholic and Eastern Orthodox followers accept a varying number of these books or portions of them as part of their Bible. They view the Apocrypha as being of equal inspiration and authority as the books in what we know as the Hebrew Bible. Jewish tradition does not recognize these other books as canonical. Protestants follow the Hebrew canon. For Protestants, the Apocrypha is like an appendix for supplement to the Old Testament.

The Canon of the New Testament
The Hebrew Bible

The Christian church inherited its Old Testament from Judaism, even though Christianity arose before the third section of the Hebrew Bible (The Writings) was canonized in the first and second centuries A.D. The early Christians accepted the Hebrew Bible, as well as some books of the Apocrypha, as sacred. They constantly quoted this Scripture to prove their message about Jesus Christ.

Also, Jesus had accepted the books of Hebrew Scripture as a true revelation. Jesus said that he had not come to abolish the Law and the Prophets but to fulfill them (Matthew 5:17). For these reasons the early Christian church retained the Hebrew Bible as its own sacred literature.

Paul's Letters

The first part of the New Testament that was written down was the letters of Paul. When Paul wrote the letters, he probably never intended them to become Scripture. Most of his letters were written to a specific church to deal with their local problems and needs. Except possibly for Romans, the letters were not intended for general circulation. Paul's letters, however, soon circulated among local churches.

Gradually, people gathered Paul's letters into a collection and began to circulate them on a wider basis. We do not know who first put them together into a collection. Some scholars suggest that the author of Ephesians collected and published nine of Paul's letters and wrote Ephesians under Paul's name as an introduction to the collection. Scholars agree that the earliest collection of Paul's letters was put together before the end of the first century. After that, Christians quickly put the collection into general use.

The Words of Jesus

Jesus did not write down his teachings. But, for early Christians, the sayings of Jesus carried high authority. These sayings were transmitted by word of mouth, memorized by Jesus' followers, and passed on to others. These spoken words of Jesus carried the seed of the New Testament before the words were ever written down. When the Gospels finally were written down, they were not considered holy books but books that contained holy words.

The Gospels

The Gospels contain the sayings, teachings, and actions of Jesus. The sources for the Gospels went through more than a generation of oral transmission before the Gospels were written down. Our New Testament contains four Gospels, but these were not the only gospels written. However, even after the gospels were written, the early church preferred oral reports from some living person who had had contact with disciples of the apostles.

After the collections of the sayings of Jesus and the stories about Jesus were written down, they began to circulate locally. Justin Martyr, who died in A.D. 165, indicated that portions of these collections were read on Sundays, as were portions from the Hebrew Bible called the Prophets.

The four Gospels that we have in the New Testament are from the second generation of Christians. They date from about A.D. 70 to 100. Mark was written first, perhaps in Rome. A few years later, the writers of Matthew and Luke used a form of Mark as a source for their Gospels. But writers of gospels felt free to add stories from their unique sources, as well as to subtract, shorten, or change the words and phrases. They sometimes even changed the order of what happened.

Why, since there were so many gospels, did the Christian church finally decide on just four as Scripture? The gospels that were rejected added nothing significant to what was already known about Jesus. Some provided distorted views of Jesus. Some were imaginative fictional tales of Jesus' birth and childhood. None of the rejected gospels ever circulated as widely as the four Gospels that finally became part of the New Testament.

Other Writings

Besides the Gospels and the collected letters of Paul, a large number of other Christian writings were produced: letters, sermons, apocalypses, manuals of teaching, and accounts of the acts of apostles. Some of these writings eventually became part of the New Testament. Others were rejected as Scripture. Some of the rejected writings have survived and are known as "The Apostolic Fathers."

Our Bible Comes Together

By the middle of the second century A.D., the church had a rich collection of writings, but none of them was treated as Holy Scripture on the same level as Scripture inherited from Judaism. The words of Jesus, whether oral or written, carried more authority than any other oral traditions or writings. The writings became Scripture through a gradual process of usage and official decision.

Generally, the church used three standards to select the writings it considered authoritative and which it finally canonized:
1. the extent of acceptance and use of a particular writing in the church;
2. the faithfulness of the writing to the church's traditional teaching; and
3. the writing having been written or authorized by an apostle.

During the second half of the second century the Gospels began to be quoted as Holy Scripture by church writers and to be used as Scripture in worship. Christians also treated Paul's letters and other writings in the same way. Churches read them alongside or in place of the Hebrew Bible.

The next step in the process was to combine Paul's letters with the Gospels. This step first was taken by Marcion, who was rejected later as a heretic. He put the collection of Paul's ten letters together with the Gospel of Luke. Though he changed some things and omitted others, his canon was the first canon of the New Testament that we know of. All later canons were based on what he began. In reaction to Marcion's work, the church began to think of a canon of books of the New Testament, rather than of a series of additions to the body of Jewish Scripture.

From A.D. 140 to 200, the authority of most of the rest of the books of the New Testament began to be accepted widely. Around the end of the second century, Irenaeus, Tertullian, and Clement of Alexandria agreed on the authority of our four Gospels, thirteen letters of Paul, Acts, 1 Peter, 1 John, and the Revelation to John. The Eastern Church, however, contested the authority of the Revelation to John. No agreement had yet been reached on the rest of the New Testament.

Around A.D. 325, Eusebius tried to distinguish between approved, unapproved, and disputed books. James, Jude, 2 Peter, and 2 and 3 John were among the disputed writings, along with other writings that were eventually rejected.

Several church councils fixed the list of books that are now in our New Testament. Important in this process were the councils held in Rome in 382, at Hippo in 393, and at Carthage in 397 and 419. Some parts of the church continued to dispute the inclusion of Revelation and some of the general Epistles until the beginning of the ninth century A.D.

From oral traditions, to writings, to collections, to use in liturgy and teaching, to official canonization by recognized religious councils—it took more than a thousand years for the Bible to take its form as we know it today.

From Teacher in the Church Today, *July 1991, pages 12-15. Copyright © 1991 by Graded Press.*

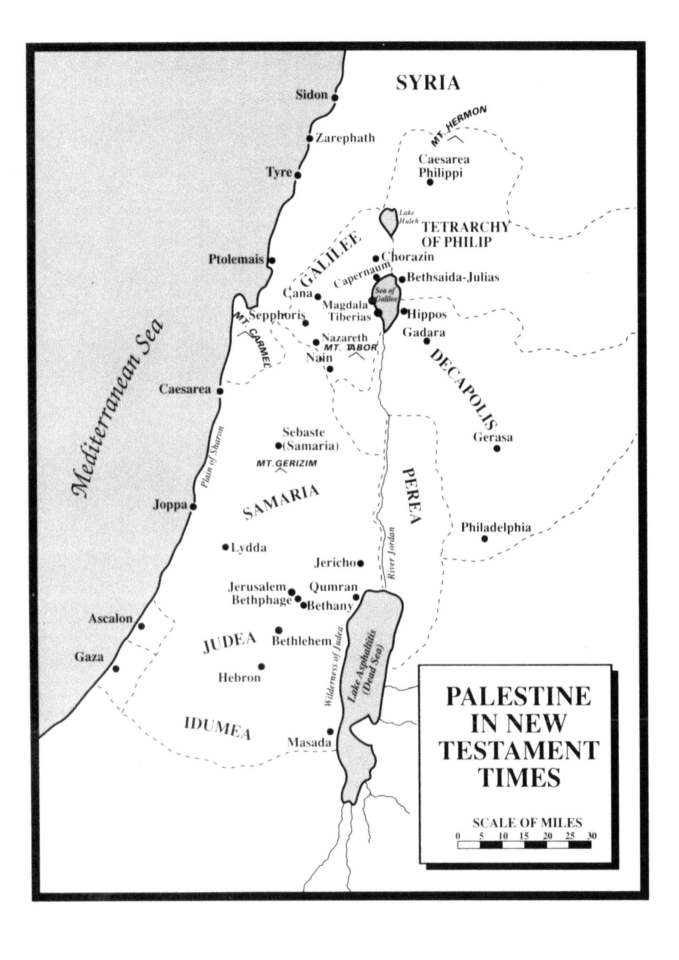

SYRIA

Sidon

Zarephath

Tyre

MT. HERMON

Caesarea
Philippi

Lake
Huleh

TETRARCHY
OF PHILIP

GALILEE

Ptolemais

Chorazin

Capernaum

Bethsaida-Julias

Cana

Magdala

Sea of
Galilee

Tiberias

Hippos

Sepphoris

Nazareth

Gadara

MT. CARMEL

MT. TABOR

Nain

DECAPOLIS

Mediterranean Sea

Caesarea

Sebaste
(Samaria)

Gerasa

MT. GERIZIM

PEREA

Plain of Sharon

Joppa

SAMARIA

Philadelphia

River Jordan

Lydda

Jericho

Jerusalem

Qumran

Bethphage

Bethany

Ascalon

JUDEA

Bethlehem

Lake
Asphaltitis
(Dead Sea)

Wilderness of Judea

Gaza

Hebron

IDUMEA

Masada

**PALESTINE
IN NEW
TESTAMENT
TIMES**

SCALE OF MILES

0   5   10 15 20 25 30

CPSIA information can be obtained
at www.ICGtesting.com
Printed in the USA
LVHW060138280922
729437LV00002B/1